Bullying Ends Here

My Story

Tad Milmine

with Leslie Robinson

Thank you for your support. Stay Amazing

Be the change!

Leslie

BULLYING
ENDS HERE

Library and Archives Canada Cataloguing in Publication

Milmine, Tad, 1974 – and Robinson, Leslie, 1953-
      Bullying ends here – my story / Tad Milmine with Leslie Robinson

Includes bibliographic references.
ISBN: 978-1-926964-14-0

Published by Quantum Learning, Calgary, Canada

I dedicate this book to
Jamie Hubley and Adrian Oliver.

Although I never had the honour of meeting Jamie,
I feel as though he is here with me.
His story inspired me to start with myself
and create change.

Adrian was one of my best friends
who died in the line of duty
protecting and serving the very same people that
I promised to protect and serve in Surrey BC.
Adrian was so proud of the work I was doing.

Tad

I dedicate this book to
my children and grandchildren
and their future generations,
that they will live in a world
of respect, kindness, and love.
I follow your lead.

Leslie

Table of Contents

The intent of this book is to share Tad's story about being bullied, how he rose above it, and how he hopes to inspire others in similar situations to do the same for themselves. Much of Tad's story has been well documented in the media. The intent is to record the events in Tad's life from HIS perspective and is not to discredit anyone else. To that end, efforts have been made to omit names, locations and relationships where possible.

Foreword

Tad's story is one that I don't wish any child to have to go through, although he has come out of it with amazing strength and integrity. I hope that anyone who reads Tad's story will be able to take something out of it, and do something positive with their life.

To the readers, I would like to say that there is a light at the end of the tunnel, and anyone can accomplish anything they put their mind to.

To the kids, I would like to tell them that Tad knows what it's like to be bullied, and have the feeling that no one loves or cares about them. They're not alone. For one, Tad is always there to listen, and he cares about each and every one of the kids that email him.

To the parents, keep an open mind when your kids try to talk to you. It might seem like a small issue to you, but it could be very important and lifesaving to the child. Listening and being active in a child's life is so important, especially these days.

To the teachers, listen to the kids, and get them help if needed, whether it's getting in touch with the parents, or other agencies that might be able to help.

Tad is honest, funny, caring, giving, and most of all, sincere.

Tad's story needs to be heard, and I'm sure most people will be able to relate to some of the stories in the book, and become more aware of what's happening in the world today.

Debbie Schmidt, Tad's Mom
7 January 2015

Tad at nine months

Tad at five years

Home

Screaming. There was always screaming. There were so many arguments, vicious arguments, I just wanted to hide. I wanted to be invisible.

There was never a time that I felt I was physically in danger. It wasn't like that. I just couldn't stand the screaming and I couldn't stand their hatred of one another. The house was a disaster. We destroyed the place. The small awning roof off my bedroom window was full of my toys. There were no repercussions when I threw them there so I did. There was a large hole in my bedroom wall where the doorknob got stuck. The house was a shambles.

My parents were young and had parties all the time. I liked it when they were blasting music, singing and dancing. I loved watching poker and card games at the dining room table. I felt happy and safe. But when the parties ended, it was nasty. My parents were cruel to one another. There was pushing, shoving, and always screaming. There were no rules. They argued and I just wanted to be alone. I wanted to hide. I wanted to be invisible.

I was always being told "Tad, go upstairs" or "Tad, come over here." I felt like I was being dragged around everywhere. I hated hearing my name and being pulled out of my hiding spot. As my mom went upstairs, it was "Tad, get up here." When my dad went outside, he said "Tad, you're coming with me." I felt like I was in the middle of my parents' tug-of-war.

I didn't understand why they were so mean to each other. She was my mom. He was my dad. I loved them both so much and all I felt was tension. I felt everything. I felt like they didn't love each other. From my perspective, it meant that they didn't love me. I somehow felt like I was the cause or I was going to get hurt. It was bad.

We didn't have much back then. We were really struggling. A car got repossessed and our food was basic like macaroni and cheese. We ate on the couches in the living room. We never sat outside or at the dinner table.

I remember the night my mom left. There was a huge argument and I heard her say "I'm leaving." She was bawling. She slammed the door. It was late at night and dark outside. Then it was just my dad and I, sitting on my dad's lap watching television. It was a different world.

The next night she called. My dad handed me the phone and my mom said "I'm not coming home anymore." I didn't understand. What did that mean? Anymore like tonight or…? I wanted them to be together. I wanted them to be happy. I wanted to be with both my mom and my dad.

I would never have known that it would basically be 10 or 15 years until I would see her again on a regular basis. Who would have thought that phone call was going to be it? I just didn't get it and was afraid to ask. I didn't want to see their anger again. I didn't want to be disappointed. The separation eventually moved to divorce. It was all the same to me. Either way, my mom was not coming home. My dad and I stayed in that house and my mom was gone.

It was so sudden and very frightening. Bit by bit, it hit me that she was not coming back. If I'd had a choice between my mom being 'gone' and their screaming, I would have picked screaming. At least they would both be here. At least they would be together.

My dad had a Monday to Friday job, so he was home at night. On weekends I saw my mom. My grandparents, my fathers' parents, lived nearby so I spent a lot of time at their place.

My dad was terrific. He liked to have a good time, he liked his parties. He was a very positive, happy man. He was always laughing, smiling, never frustrated, and he always had the time of day for me. Always!

He played a lot of baseball, so we went to the parks and I watched his baseball games and explored the park. I loved being a part of it whether I was picking up a baseball bat or helping tidy up at the end. I always hoped we'd get together afterwards. I'd ask my dad "Is the team going to a restaurant? Is the team coming back to our house?" I wanted us to all stay together.

Over the next several years, we spent a lot of time at my grandparents' home. They played a big role in making me feel safe, especially as time went on. My grandfather had been in the war and was a severe alcoholic. He never left the living room. He lay on the couch all day, every day. He lay there for so long that eventually he couldn't walk anymore. He was confined to a wheelchair because he didn't use his legs. He had several drinks of choice but mostly it was hard alcohol, rum and diet Coke. He was obnoxious and mean, screaming at my grandmother to "Give me my food" or "Get me a drink" or "I want ketchup". It was nonstop.

For whatever reason, I loved my grandfather and I would always go into the living room to watch police shows together. One of our favourite shows was *T.J. Hooker*. We didn't talk much when we watched it. It was really tough for my grandfather to speak. He gurgled his words which was probably part medical and part intoxication. Later, when *T.J. Hooker* got pulled from the air, my grandfather was the one to tell me. I stood in front of him, crying. *T.J. Hooker* was our thing and now it, too, was gone.

My grandmother was the sweetest, kindest, most incredible woman anyone could ever meet. She was always, always there. She loved me to bits. She bought me a little red barn toy that was probably twenty years old even then. I loved to play with the little barn doors, the people and the animals. Every Sunday night, she made roast beef, mashed potatoes and corn. Sometimes it was creamed corn, other times just regular corn. I still remember those smells. She went all out. She was the most loving, supportive person around and I think she played a large role in helping me get through what was happening. Having that stability around me made the world a little better.

My grandmother and I went everywhere together. She took me for my first ride on a public bus. She took me on my first escalator. I remember watching the stairs appear and disappear. I was nervous to get on. Her hand was wrinkled, strong and so much bigger than mine. She held my left hand warmly as we went down to the pet section at the bottom of the escalator. I loved looking in the aquariums.

She was so proud to show me off. She'd take me to the Salvation Army and introduce me to all the people there and she'd always buy me the penny or five-cent candy, just 'a little something'.

Our Christmases were very basic. I don't remember any stockings but they had an artificial tree. She had a beautiful wooden cabinet full of dishes and antiques. My favourite decorations were the Mr. and Mrs. Claus salt and pepper shakers sitting on a little bench.

There were two boys about my age who lived near us. I always went to their house, they never came to mine. They had a model train set that their dad had built in their basement rec room. The rec room had a couch and carpeted floors and two tables where we played house. I would be the visitor and I'd go visit one boy and then I'd go visit the other boy. We fondled and caressed and held each other. We were visiting, you know? One was definitely receptive, the other not so much. It was nothing serious, just kids exploring and learning. It all felt very normal. I saw them every day.

We never went to the basement in our house. We were told that there was a man in a straight-jacket who lived down there. I don't know where that came from but I was always petrified of our basement.

I was slowly becoming introverted. I was afraid to say anything to upset someone so I started going into my shell. The day my mom left was divorce to me. I stuck to what I was comfortable with and I trusted those two boys, my grandparents and my dad.

Shortly after mom called and said she wasn't coming home anymore, another woman moved into the house. I wasn't keen on her presence since it cemented the fact that my mom was gone and she was not coming back.

There was something about her that I never liked. When she moved into our house, she and my dad argued a lot and I went back to hiding. Soon after she moved in, we moved out of that house to another house close to my grandparents.

She—'that woman' as I call her now—always said "kids don't belong upstairs." She set up a room in the new basement with a two-seater couch, a wooden table and a little black television with rabbit ears. There was no heat and no air conditioning. I went to school, came home, went to the basement, then went up to bed at 9pm. That became my life for years.

At first, we ate upstairs together. As their relationship became more strained, they became very, very rough—even rougher than when my parents were together. There was even more screaming and a lot of physical grabbing and holding.

She did a lot of hitting. Food was put on a plate at the top of the stairs and I was left alone in the basement.

When she came into our lives, baseball with my dad stopped. It was gone. Whether it was his doing, or hers, I didn't know, but I always blamed her for him not playing baseball as much. It also meant I wasn't getting out of the house anymore.

After one of the last ball games, my dad and I went to a friends' house and they were drinking. I loved when the adults drank because they were happy. The phone kept ringing. It was 'that woman' saying "When are you coming home?" My dad kept saying "just one more drink." He was drinking his liquor and they were playing cards. It was fun. Quite frankly, neither of us wanted to go home. When we finally did, she dumped a pot of macaroni and cheese over my head. My dad told me to go to the basement and the screaming began. It was out of control.

I sat at the top of the stairs and peeked through the opening. My dad called her parents and said "Come over here, come get her. Can you talk to her please?" There was nothing he could do to stop her. She ripped the phone right off the wall. There was more screaming and sounds of things breaking. I heard slapping too. It was awful. That was one of the nights that my dad packed us up in the cold and we spent the night at my grandparent's house.

She was the bad person that time. Other times, I was told that she was the good person. It was confusing. For me, she was always the bad person who made me go to the basement. It was cold and I was lonely. I was becoming the little boy who couldn't speak to people.

My mom had visitation rights and picked me up every other Saturday night after *Solid Gold* was on TV. But some nights, she didn't. One night, I sat at the front door step waiting for her. She didn't come. Of course, it was before we had cell phones or emails. 'That woman' thought it was funny and said "She doesn't love you. Now, get back down to the basement."

I was emotionally destroyed because mom hadn't picked me up. I had been excited to see her and to get out of the basement, and now I had 'that woman' saying "Get back down to the basement."

I didn't know why then, but I do know now. My mom wasn't in a place to be a mom. She worked in bars and Friday and Saturday nights were her big nights. When she did come, she dropped me at a baby sitter and went to work. at 2 or 3 in the morning, she bundled me up in a snow suit and put me in the back seat of the car still half asleep. I hated it, but that was the best she could do.

I had always liked it when the adults drank, but when we moved into the new house, the drinking wasn't happy anymore. I think my dad drank to the point where he hoped the problems would go away. He never addressed it. That's when I first started thinking, he was drinking to prevent himself for standing up for himself, or me, or locking me in the basement, or to tell her to stop screaming'.

So for me, alcohol wasn't fun anymore. Alcohol was distracting him from helping me. He was drinking all the time. Whenever he called me upstairs, he was under the influence. He was an alcoholic. He always had a rum and diet Coke; I could smell it on him. He was glassy-eyed and had that little grin on his face. He smelled stale. Whenever his glass moved, that smell would waft

Alcoholism never affected my dad's work; it was a nighttime thing. He was a highly functioning alcoholic. He would never agree to that, but he was. He didn't call in sick to work, but he drank every single night.

The drinking was not fun anymore, but his demeanor towards me never changed. He was still loving, caring, kind, nurturing in the moments that we had together. Every night, we hugged and kissed when I went to bed, and so it was all the way until the end.

I was always scared of 'that woman'. There was only one washroom, on the main floor. If I was in the basement and had to go to the washroom, I would find some place in that basement to pee. Sometimes it was the laundry sink or a floor drain. I peed there. I did everything possible not to have to go upstairs. I was absolutely petrified of her.

When I was in my bedroom, I had to go downstairs past 'that woman' to get to the washroom. I was so terrified of her, I peed out the window instead. I did that all the time; just peed out of the window. When summer came and it got hot, I tried to clean it up to hide the smell.

Around this time, the two boys I played with moved away. They were my world. I don't remember them packing up and moving. I just remember that, all of a sudden, they were gone. I missed them and felt so alone.

My grandmother was aware because I was in tears all the time. She cuddled me. She always took me to the kitchen where she had little biscuits she kept in a wooden bread box. She gave me little pats on the head. I was never pushed away when I was there. I was included in everything.

At my own house, I always felt pushed away. I wasn't included, except one day every summer. The stepdad of 'that woman' gave me one day a year to plan a trip wherever we wanted to go, just him and I. Often times, we went to Canada's Wonderland and one time we went to Detroit. I'd never been to the Unites States before and remember driving across the bridge. He put in a Bruce Springsteen tape, *Born in the USA*, and I sang away with him. He was the one man in my life who I knew just loved me. I knew it.

I knew that my grandmother and grandfather loved me, but they weren't able to do the things that he was able to do. He was much more financially stable. He was just an incredible man. Everybody loved him.

There were no family vacations I can recall. There were no extraordinary gifts at Christmas. Any good memories were from being out of the house on Christmas Eve. The stepdad of 'that woman' took me to church where we sang Christmas carols then went back to his house and had meatballs. The smell of Christmas in the air was very festive, everyone was drinking. It was magical. I loved being out of the house, out of the basement, and, for a short while away, from the dirty secret behind the four walls of my home. Everyone was happy. For me, Christmas Eve is still special. Christmas Day is another day to me. It was always stressful. It wasn't fun.

Somehow, growing up, I thought everyone knew that I was locked in the basement and someday, someone would come and rescue me. The immediate neighbors must have known because 'that woman' screamed so loudly. It still makes me angry. I heard it all the time. Both sets of grandparents knew, but no one did anything. Christmas Eve was a magical escape, but then the reality would come back for the other 364 days of the year.

In the basement, I just daydreamed and watched the little TV with the rabbit ears. We got CBC and, luckily for me, the Blue Jays played almost every day, nine months out of the year. The Blue Jays are very special to me. They feel like my best friends. Blue Jay games were three hours long plus an hour before and an hour after. I had a binder with loose lined paper and every game I wrote down the date, the team played, where they played, who had home runs, who had RBIs, anything else of note. I did this every day. I had eight binders, one for every year I watched the Blue Jays in that basement.

I avoided 'that woman' at all costs. When I heard creaking floorboards upstairs, I knew she was coming down. I hated that sound. If I was lying down, I sat up. I always said "Hi" or something. I could tell if she was in a mood or not from the tone in her voice. I was so afraid of her.

I had few toys. I made a couple of model cars and glued together the little bits. It was great for me because it took a lot of time. I had something to do.

In the basement, I dreamed of being a police officer. Oh, just to drive in a police car, wearing a uniform, not being afraid. It had a good feeling, that sense of nothing to be afraid of anymore. Whenever I heard a siren, or saw a police vehicle or a police officer, I stared in awe. I wanted to know what they were doing, where they were going. I imagined that I was with them, in that moment, wearing that uniform and helping people. It was a dream that started at a young age and that dream grew with every passing day.

I don't remember ever thinking anything beyond being a police officer. I didn't dream about a house or who would I live with; I just fixated on being a police officer. I was glued to police TV shows. Like the Blue Jays, they were my escape. I saw myself in the shows. TV was a way of holding a better future for myself. It helped me block out what was going on in my house.

I felt like a stew, all mixed up. I knew things were wrong in my house. I knew I was in a bad spot. I knew there was no foreseeable way out, and every day I felt more powerless. I felt like the light at the end of the tunnel was getting dimmer and dimmer until I couldn't see it anymore. I was depressed.

One night, *T.J. Hooker* was on TV and I wanted to watch it. They had cable upstairs and I had to pass 'that woman' to be able to tune in. My heart was beating out of my chest as I stopped at the top of the stairs. The door, of course, was closed. Sometimes the door was closed but not locked, but for me the door was always locked. I knocked on the door and 'that woman' answered. I was so nervous I could barely use my words. It took all the courage in the world for me to say "May I please watch T.J. Hooker up here?" I remember the exact tone of her voice when she said "There's no need for you to be upstairs tonight" and that was it. My dad never said anything, so back downstairs I went. I was crushed.

My dad and I had a nightly ritual. 'That woman' always went to bed early. I heard her footsteps going up to their bedroom. I waited 10 minutes and then I heard my dad's footsteps on the floor above me walking from the living room to the basement door. He fumbled with the lock as he unlocked the basement door and said "Hey you, come upstairs now" and I went upstairs.

There was an afghan on the couch. It was gray and burgundy. My dad laid on the couch with the afghan draped over him. He curled his legs up over me and I wrapped the afghan around me and then we watched TV for half an hour or an hour. We always whispered. If we heard any stirring upstairs, I darted back downstairs. We didn't want her to know I was upstairs. That was part of the dirty little secret. We were sure she knew, but, we kept it on the down low. We were both afraid of her. Even when my dad came down to the basement, we kept quiet.

I was changing emotionally. Any time there was any type of fear, sadness, or disappointment, I cried. I hyperventilated. Boogers came out my nose, my shoulders shook. It really took hold of me. I could never speak. It didn't matter how hard I tried, I couldn't get a word out. Emotionally, I was out of control.

Occasionally, on a Sunday, my dad and I visited family friends. They had a son who was double my age, somewhere between twelve and sixteen. The adults told us to 'go play' and so we went downstairs to their basement fully furnished basement with a games room.

There was a ping-pong table. We bent the table at the seam in the middle and tucked a blanket down there to divide the underside of the table, put the table back down and then draped blankets all around the edges to make two houses. There was a big rack of canned foods in the room. We took all the canned food off the shelves and threw them into our respective houses and started visiting one to the other.

I don't remember how it developed, but one day it turned sexual. He forced sexual acts on me. My pants were around my ankles. We didn't get naked because we were both hypersensitive to the adults upstairs. If they came down, we had to get clothes on. Whatever he said to do, I did it. I didn't understand it. I didn't like it. I was the victim. I just wanted to be invisible.

I didn't want to disappoint or upset him. I always felt like I was disappointing someone. Everywhere I went, it seemed someone was either pissed off, disappointed, mad or simply hated me. In some weird way, he was showing affection. I didn't know it was wrong. I just knew it was happening. I liked that I was getting some kind of attention even though that sounds very confused. It was painful and not. It wasn't enjoyable or pleasurable or anything. There was nothing I could do.

One time, I was lying on my stomach, my pants down around my ankles with my backside fully exposed. He stood up while I was lying down and he peed all over my back. He laughed. I thought it was gross. When he was done, the adults called downstairs. "Have you guys cleaned up down there?" We quickly tidied up, put the food back on the shelves and pulled the blankets off the ping-pong table. He looked at me soaking wet and said "You stink and the basement's going to stink". He got the box of Tide, the powdered form, and sprinkled Tide all over me. He was laughing. I guess he thought I was just going to smell like fresh laundry. I remember thinking this was the solution, this was going to fix it. I toweled off and pulled my pants back up just like nothing had happened. The adults never knew what was going on. I certainly didn't tell anyone.

I didn't have to go with my dad to that house, but the alternative was to stay in the basement alone with 'that woman' upstairs. I chose to go with my dad, knowing where we were going and what was probably going happen. As I left the house, the first thing I wondered was "Is he home?" I know there were times he was sleeping in after partying the night before. When he woke up, the adults said "Okay guys, go downstairs". The adults didn't think twice about a six, seven or eight-year-old boy sitting in the living room with them while they were drinking, smoking and partying. It was just "Tad, go play downstairs." So I went to the basement with him.

I had zero control. There was nothing I could do to stop it. There was no one I could talk to. If I spoke up, who would believe me? Besides, at that age, we didn't speak about sexual acts, whether same sex, opposite sex, or sex in general. I was young; I didn't even know what sex was.

It was always very brief. It was a very quick thing and then we just went on with whatever we're doing. I didn't despise him. I wasn't afraid of him. I can't say that I enjoyed him or looked forward to seeing him. I just knew there weren't any hard negative feelings either. Even when that act was over, we still had to get along because we were in that basement together.

I don't remember how it ever stopped. It's not like we ever decided to stop. It was just like baseball—one day we just stopped going to that house and that was the end of it. Gone.

One evening, my dad, 'that woman,' my real mother and her husband met at a local restaurant. My mother was now in a place where she was ready to have one of the boys and they felt it was in my brother's best interest if he went to live with her. My brother was struggling even more than me in the house.

When my dad and 'that woman' came back to the house, they told my brother and I that he was going to be going to live with Mom and to pack up all his toys. I was eight and he was five. We were in the basement, of course, and his stuffed animals were in a tall cupboard. I was much taller so I pulled out his stuffed animals and he held the garbage bag. We worked at Mach speed. I remember saying "Get out, get out while you can." He was crying and I'm sure I was as well.

I thought, "How fortunate for him, he gets to escape the house and he's going to go live with Mom." To us, Mom was the 'golden world.' We never really saw her, we just had this image that it was a great place. Out the door he went. My brother was gone. I really didn't see him again for years. We never got the opportunity to know each other or be brothers.

When he was gone, I sat on the couch in the basement and thought "I don't have to share this couch with anybody anymore." Somehow, it was relief, both positive and negative. Negative because I was still there and positive because now it was just my space. Then I realized, now it was just me, alone in the basement. My brother was gone.

After my brother left, I became more and more shy. I had become so introverted, I struggled to even saying "Hello."

Even if someone said "Hi" or was just being a friend, I had no idea how to interact with them. I didn't know how to reply.

Bullying started between the ages of eight and ten. At first it was pretty much just names and na, na, na, na; very immature young things. As I got older it became more personal, more hurtful, and more complicated to sort out. I just didn't know what was going on in my life. Everything seemed negative, nothing seemed positive. There never seemed to be anything to look forward to.

While all that was going on, I knew that my relationships with boys were definitely more intense than with girls. I didn't understand it. I knew my eyes looked more towards the boys who started playing a bigger role in my life. My mind raced trying to understand it but I never had anyone to talk to, or computers to look things up. Everything was just so confusing. There were big struggles for sure.

We bought a new house on the other side of the river. We weren't renting anymore. I started a new school and walked into the classroom where everyone was sitting on the floor in a circle. The teacher introduced me. Everyone was so nice. The teacher was nice; the classroom was nice; the kids were nice… our house was nice too but it had a basement.

The new basement had four cement walls and a concrete floor. The whole basement was open except for a concrete alcove to store tin cans. There were windows with a big draft coming in. We boarded up one window to keep out the draft. There was no heat and no air conditioning in the summer. It was always freezing down there.

I had a small rug that was light beige with brown lines. I had a Tonka truck and I used those lines on the carpet as my roads. For hours, I drove this little truck around, backing it up, opening the doors and dumping out all the little toys I had in it. I used the tall cupboard where my brother's stuffed animals had been as my toy cabinet. It had a pull door and there were two drawers. I put my toys away every night. I had to.

Everything had to be spotless at all times. She said it was not a play room. It was my room, period. There was one screw-in light bulb in the ceiling. The washing machine, the dryer, the freezer and a fridge down were down there. There was more in this basement than before. That meant there was more reason for her to come downstairs. My room was directly below the living room so I heard every step. With every step, my anxiety went up. Again there was a lock on the door. It was just a small clasp lock but to me it was a bank vault. Even though I could probably have broken that lock with one finger, I didn't dare. Anytime I went upstairs in that house, I had to pass her on the couch. There was no way of avoiding her.

My bedroom was tiny, which was good for me. I liked small, confined spaces—they were comforting. The bedroom had to be spotless at all times. There was a desk, a single bed, a cardboard night stand with a charcoal brown drape, an alarm clock and a lamp. I had a low window where I could look outside and watch the kids laughing and playing, having fun. I wondered what it would be like being out after dinner throwing a ball around or playing hide and seek or whatever the kids on the street were doing.

'That woman' selected the clothes for me to wear each day. She took my clothes out of the closet and put them on a certain spot on the floor.

At least twice, my dad drank to excess and mixed up my bedroom with the washroom. He came into my room and peed in the corner where my clothes were. 'That woman' knew which clothes she had selected and I was too afraid to ask her to change them. I wore the clothes to school the next day.

When I had a bath, I had to use the dirty water. There was no shower for me. My dad typically had the first bath and then I had his bath water. Sometimes my dad had his bath, then she had her bath, and finally I had mine. Either way, I always bathed in dirty water.

In the basement was a fridge. It was always stocked full of Labatt Blue and Diet Coke. That was my dad's drink. Because I was too afraid to go upstairs, I drank whatever was in the fridge. In this new house, I peed in the laundry sink.

I dreaded the school bell at the end of every day. It meant I had to go home and home, for me, meant straight to the basement.

'That woman' was always there. My crying really kicked in and she recognized it. She called me names like cry baby and sucky baby. She laughed when I cried. She yelled when I cried. Because I could not speak when I was crying, she screamed at me. It was a daily ritual; every day when I got home from school, in the same way, using the same words. She stood at the top of the stairs and I was in the basement around the corner, bawling. She screamed at top of her lungs. Everyone could hear her, there's no way people didn't. My dad wasn't home from work yet, so I felt extra vulnerable. I thought, "Hurry up dad, come home," but I knew he wasn't going to stop it anyway.

Around this time, I realized there was only one thing I wanted from her. I wanted her to like me. I didn't care about love. I just wanted her to like me for a few minutes. I did everything to win her admiration. I cleaned the basement, I painted the basement, I put away all my toys. She just kept yelling and screaming about how was I was messing up their marriage. She always said that to me. Everything just kept building.

Tad 14 years

Tad 16 years

School

By grades five and six, I was crying uncontrollably at school. I knew I wasn't like the other kids. I didn't gel with them and I didn't play sports. In Phys. Ed., I hated picking teams. I was so shy. I didn't have any friends and no one knew me so I was always one of the last picked. I was being bullied at home and now it was happening at school too. When the kids at school realized they could make me cry by calling me names, the bullying at school really intensified. It was just like at home.

My marks were less of a concern to my teachers than to me, taking my report card home. 'That woman' always knew when I had a test or a project. My marks were usually in the high 60s, low 70s, which was enough for her to scream at me. When I got home, I went to the basement, and slid the test or report card under the door. Within moments, I heard the scuffling of footsteps on the floor. I waited thirty seconds while she looked at it. I heard pages flipping, the house was so quiet, and then the screaming would start. Not that screaming was ever going to help me get better grades, but that was what she did.

In grade 6 we had an exchange teacher from Great Britain. She was incredible. She was on vacation teaching in a different country and I remember having some really good chats with her. She was a person I felt safe with. She was kind and she smiled at me, and asked me how I was doing. She made me feel special but I couldn't tell her about being locked in the basement or that I was increasingly interested in boys and what could I do about both things.

We always had our desks in groups of six. I always asked to move my desk to the corner. I just wanted to be away from people. I wanted to be left alone. I didn't trust them, I didn't like them, I was afraid of them.

The walk to and from school was twenty minutes each way. I walked by myself; at least it felt like I walked by myself, even though there were kids walking in front and behind me. It was an assembly line walking the same way every day. I was always sad because I didn't have anything to do but go straight home to the basement.

There was one day that was different. On my way to school, I stopped into a corner store and stole a chocolate bar. I wanted the treat and had no other means to get it. I wasn't alone when I took the chocolate bar but I took responsibility for it. The storekeeper walked me to the school driveway. The principal grabbed my wrist and asked what I did at the store. Right away I said, "I stole a chocolate bar" and he said "Let's go to my office". Now I was in trouble with someone else. A feeling of dread came over me. That's what I was used to. I was always disappointing people. I was always making people mad. I went to the principal's office and he called the police. I was afraid of the police officer because I knew I had done something wrong. I didn't want to disappoint him, which, of course, I did. The police drove me home and 'that woman' was very nice to them, but as soon as they left she screamed, absolutely screamed, at me.

She called my dad at work. The belt came out and up to the bedroom we went. I know he didn't want to do it, but she was making him, saying "You spank this boy!" Over his knee I went with the belt. It was sunny outside. I could just tell from his hesitation that he didn't want to spank me but he did it anyhow. There was no arguing with her. There was certainly no standing up for me. There was no heart-to-heart father-son conversation. I wanted the chocolate bar and I didn't have the money, so I took it.

Some time later, at school, I got to be captain of the junior patrol. The exchange teacher from England recommended me for the position. It was like being a police officer for a year and it was the greatest thing. I had my own yellow vest and lined everyone up. I had a feeling of being in control, for what felt like the first time in my life. Until then, I really didn't like myself, so why would anyone else?

There was one boy that I was attracted to. He was my target. In a sense, I was a bully to him, because I liked him. I wanted to spend time with him. If I saw him on a patrol line up and he wasn't perfectly in line, I called him out saying "You, get out of line, come stand over here" and I got my chance to talk to him. He was very popular so I wasn't setting him back socially. Little did he know I was trying to say "I like you." I don't think that message ever got through though. I was struggling. I abused my power as the captain of the junior patrol because I was attracted to him and I finally had a sense of control. I was so lost in it. I didn't have the social skills from all those years in the basement and I certainly didn't know what to do about my attraction to him.

Junior high school meant another new school for me; this one was a little closer to home. I liked my homeroom teacher. He was someone I didn't know who I saw every day. I felt safe with him. He was nice. He was kind. Simple kindness was so absent in my world that when I got a bit, it really stood out for me.

Things were changing. One day, we were sitting in rows and this boy looked at me and said "You're going home tonight and…" he gave me the sign of jacking off with his hand curved and thrusting to and from his crotch. I had no idea what he was doing but I also remember going home that night and trying it out. I learned things about my body that no one taught me. There were no books, no porn, no Internet. I wanted to know what was going on with my body. It was a big deal for me. It just changed everything.

I started seeing things like the hair on my legs going higher and getting darker. Puberty was setting in. These physical changes added to my other challenges. Everything else was so messed up in my life, I was afraid my body might let me down. There's a big difference between grade 6 and grade 7. I was getting older and so were the bullies.

The bullies, in the new school, caught on quickly that they could make me cry. They called me names under their breath so only I could hear it. They knocked books out of my hands and hip-checked me into my locker. I cried. I was a slobber fest. I lost it. This happened many times a day.

I was so ashamed and did everything I could to hide my crying. I covered my eyes. I pulled my hoodie over my head. I looked down. In a weird way, my reactions to their bullying made me an accomplice to their bullying. They bullied me and I hid it. It was all done in secret. I just wanted to be left alone.

People thought I was happy because I smiled a lot. I was always very positive whenever I was speaking in class. I didn't communicate unless it was absolutely necessary and when I did, I appeared to be very happy. It was another way of hiding.

At home, we were much better off. Financially, my dad was in a good job. He was making more money. 'That woman' was a stay-at-home woman and kept the house pristine.

My chores were all the outside. I was in charge of taking out the garbage, cutting the grass, weeding the yard, trimming the edges. There were flowers everywhere. We had a pretty big yard so it took me at least an hour just to cut the grass. It looked great and I knew I had done a good job but there were never any compliments. It just didn't happen. As long as the grass was cut, she didn't scream. I was in her good books for a little while at least. In winter, I shoveled the driveway. When we got a snowstorm, I shoveled every chance I got just to be outside.

My dad stayed consistent with me the whole time. He still unlocked the door every night when she went up to bed and we watched TV together. Sometimes, when she screamed down at me from the top of the stairs, he brought his drink down to the basement where I was bawling. He told me, "Just ignore her, Tad. She'll stop". He told me this hundreds, if not thousands, of times growing up. He said it quietly, almost in a whisper, which set her off even more. But then, he was able to escape. He walked right by her and sat in the living room while she maintained her consistent screaming in my direction. That was the closest he ever came to fixing the situation. I never understood why he didn't stop it.

I was getting to an age where I knew what was right and wrong. Up until then, I tried to ignore her as my dad said. As I grew from a boy into a young man, I kept wondering about why she screamed and why he did nothing to stop it and why was this happening to me. Emotionally I was very young and yet I had a growing curiosity about what was really happening and why.

At first I thought something was wrong with me. I sucked it up. That didn't work. She kept screaming at me, "Stop crying, you effing, blah, blah, blah!" I kept beating myself up emotionally thinking "Why can't I stop crying all the time?" That didn't work either. It just kept building and stayed inside. I did not reach out to teachers at school or my dad. I did not tell anyone. I just held it in.

I realized I had hit a victim mentality of not being able to tell anyone. That was the psychological hold she had on me. If I told anyone, she would know that I told and that would make it worse. I was a vault. I kept everything in and that's when things started going downhill.

By grade 8 everything was the same. My dad did the same things. She did the same things. I was still in the basement. Now, when she made a plate of food for me, she unlocked the basement door and put the plate at the top of the stairs. On those nights, I only had five minutes to eat before the yelling started. Many nights I didn't even know that there was food there. I started listening very closely to the sounds of people sitting at the dining table and hearing knives and forks cutting and scraping on the ceramic plates. When I heard that, I peeked around the corner to the top of the stairs to see if there was a plate there. I never wanted to be caught doing that. It meant even more time in the basement, even more time by myself.

Somewhere around grade 7 or 8, they had a daughter. For me, that was just yet another negative factor in the equation. She was their daughter. The rule for me was there was no place for kids upstairs but her daughter was allowed upstairs. In fact, her daughter was not allowed downstairs in the basement; upstairs only. She had play-dates. Friends came to the house and brought her presents but there was nothing for me. I was just the kid in the basement and I felt even further removed from the family.

I went to a school dance once. I liked being out of the house and people watching. I never danced. I just stood off and watched, sometimes with a teacher and mostly alone. I really didn't get the boy-girl thing. I couldn't figure out what they were doing. I felt pressure to start looking at girls, hanging out with them, and I knew I needed to get a girlfriend. I much preferred watching the boys.

Somehow, I knew there was something deeper for me with boys. My feelings were involved. It wasn't just a physical curiosity of are we the same size or anything like that. There were feelings. An attraction was there. I thought about them even when I wasn't with them. I just knew that I liked boys in a way that no one else seemed to like them. I didn't know what it was. I didn't know there was a name for it. I didn't know other people did it. There were no role models, no TV shows, no classes, no Gay Straight Alliance (GSA) club. I thought I was the only person on this planet that liked boys. I really, really did.

There was a TV show with two brothers and I was so in love with them. I couldn't wait for the show to come on every week. It was a half hour comedy series based in the living room of a house. I felt they were real and wanted them to be here with me. I wanted to get to know them. It was so weird.

I loved what I called Tad Time. Tad Time is when I get time to myself without intrusions, without yelling. It is time when everything is peaceful, quiet and I know I am safe from others, from judgment, and from falling behind in work. It is a time when I can be in my own space and thoughts. Tad Time is when I get to do what I want when I want.

I got a form of Tad Time when company came over. 'That woman' didn't scream or call me names. She didn't come downstairs except to get beer. I felt invincible. The dirty little secret stayed within the four walls of our home. As the music got louder, there was more singing, laughter and dancing. She told stories about how I was such a good boy. I guess it made her feel good about herself. For me, it was nauseating. It was false, a lie. She was drunk.

'That woman' refused to let me see my grandparents, my moms' parents. I remember times when, from the basement, I heard them knock on the front door saying "Can we please see Tad?" and she slammed the door in their faces.

There was one time, during a visit with my mom, that I went to their retirement home. My grandmother knitted me some red mittens. As she gave them to me she was crying and said, "I wish I could see you more. I could give you these gifts." Apparently my grandparents left gifts for me on the front step and 'that woman' threw them out so I never got them.

One day at home before going to school, I came out of my bedroom and 'that woman' was at the bottom of the stairs. She said, "Tad, I need to tell you something." I stood my distance. I didn't want to get down to her level so I stayed four steps up the stairs. She said "Your grandparents were killed this morning in a car crash." I was stunned. I didn't understand death. She walked away and that was it.

I went to school like a zombie. I was not allowed to go to their funeral. My mom tried to get me there to be around the family and to mourn with them. No, absolutely not. My dad came down to the basement and talked to me a bit about it. My grandparents were gone.

By Grade 8, all I had were the mother of 'that woman', her incredible stepdad, and my dads' parents. Grandma, my dad's mom, was in terrible shape. She had heart attacks all the time and was less and less mobile. She was in an assisted living home. Grandpa was still an alcoholic and snuck alcohol into the old folk's home. Sometimes on Sundays I went with my dad to see them. She never went. She hated them and wanted no part. I got to be with my dad and at the same time see my grandparents. I really wish I had spent more time with them. Now, I go to their gravesite and talk to them and kiss the tombstone. I know I'm the only person who goes. It is important to me and that's why I do it. I know it's important to them.

I loved law class. I loved my law teacher. We both loved the law and we really hit it off. I loved when he brought in guest speakers like crown council and a police officer. I idolized them.

My law teacher was genuinely interested in me and would ask me how I was. In a brief chat after school, he said he liked music. My dad had terrific music, so I offered to make him a cassette. He said "That would be nice." That day, I was alone in the living room at home. I was so nervous! I made a mixed tape for him and took it to school the next day. He thanked me. It made me feel special. I made more and more mixed tapes.

My law teacher was also a huge Blue Jays fan. When the Blue Jays won the World Series, he took a photo of the team celebrating from the front page of the Toronto Sun and burned it onto a piece of wood. He gave it to me to hang on my wall. He understood me, and now he was giving me gifts. He was a great man in a time in my life when I had no role models or even someone to be interested in me. He always seemed to have time for me.

I was in the basement, of course, on the day they bought a new fridge for upstairs and put the old one in the basement. After they set it up on the cement floor, she said "Tad, get over here." I walked over. My dad was there so I felt somewhat at ease. They told me to open the fridge. They were both standing right there. Something was up. Was something going to jump out at me? What was it?

They told me to just open it and so I did. I got an electrical shock and quickly yanked my hand off. They cracked up laughing. I tried to smirk. They exploded in laughter. I was embarrassed, ashamed, and hurt because my dad was there and knew what was going to happen. It was a total set-up. They loved my discomfort. I has trusted my dad and I had no idea about getting shocked. I would never have thought of it. I felt completely betrayed.

That day I learned that a fridge needs to be grounded. That day, I also learned that I was being bullied by my dad and 'that woman'. I was beginning to realize that even in my own house, I was a victim and I could not even trust my father.

I had held a fantasy that I was okay when I was with my dad, but this time he let me down. I had a growing realization that maybe I wasn't okay. Moments like that play into my everyday life even now. Any time I open a fridge, I'm reminded.

On my 16th birthday, I did my driving test and passed. That was a very good day. In addition to our black topaz four-door, my dad splurged and bought a silver two-door sporty car. Now I could be sent out on chores. It got me out of the house and I got to drive.

By the age of 16, I was depressed. Despite having a driver's license and a friend , I didn't have anything going on in my life to look forward to.

There was one afternoon when my dad and 'that woman' had been drinking so I pushed my luck a little bit. I had a friend down in the basement with me hanging out on my little couch. I was feeling calm and at peace knowing they were drinking upstairs. She was not screaming and she was not going to call me names with my friend there.

I heard a knock at the front door and I could tell she and my dad had answered it. I heard guffaws and laughing and voices I didn't recognize. I thought "oh wow, this is good!" Not only were they drinking but now there's company over.

This was a good day and I've got a friend with me. They were having a good time and they left me alone. I was at peace.

All of a sudden, she screamed out my name "Tad, get up here." I looked at my friend. He didn't know about what went on in my house. My anxiety went up. I walked up the stairs, the door was unlocked and I thought "there's company over so it will be all right."

On one couch directly in front of me, 'that woman' was sitting looking right at me and beside her, to my left, was my dad. On the other side of the couch were two adults that I'd never met before. She looked at the woman and said "this is Tad, the half that nobody wants." That's how she introduced me! I looked to my dad and he wasn't even with us. He was out there somewhere, no reaction whatsoever. I looked back to her and she snickered, thinking she had said something funny, and the two adults laughed as well.

I sharpened my shoulder ever so slightly, turned around and walked back downstairs. As I did, a flash of tears came. I went downstairs and my friend looked at me, mortified. "Did she just say that?" I lost it, absolutely lost it.

It was a matter of minutes before he left. He was in way over his head. He didn't know what the hell was going on. In a way, I didn't want him there for those tears but at the same time, he was my comfort and now he was leaving. What's a 14-year-old boy to do with a 16-year-old boy who's bawling? I'd get right out of there too.

My tears, my emotions were different from all those other times I cried. After 12 years of putting in effort, she was never going to like me. There was nothing more I could do. She was now being cruel to me in front of other people. She had changed it from the dirty little secret behind the four walls of our home and went public.

I lost hope that an adult would see that I was locked in the basement and save me. I wanted the knight in shining armor to rescue me. The adults upstairs could have rescued me, but they snickered with her.

I knew when she called me "the half that nobody wants," she was comparing me to my half-sister. She was the half that's sitting there having a picnic in the middle of the living room at the time on her pink blankie. My brother was the half that got to live with my mom, and here again, I was the half that nobody wanted.

Those 15 seconds were a defining moment in my life.

I knew I was suicidal right away. I also knew I didn't want to die. I had no thoughts of death. I just wanted everything to end. There's a huge difference there. I wanted her to stop screaming. I wanted her to stop laughing at me. I wanted her to stop calling me names. I just wanted her to leave me alone. At school, that's all I ever wanted from the kids. I didn't care about friendships. I didn't care about love. I just wanted to be left alone. All I did was cry. I just wanted to be invisible.

I did not reach out and ask for help. I did not go to my counselor's office. I did not go to my favourite teacher. I kept everything in and had to find a way through it. I just focused on things around me that I enjoyed like sunshine or law class. Those were the things got me through.

My friend and I never spoke about what he heard in the basement and I could feel our friendship dissolving. I knew I was falling. I realized I was falling head over heels for him, and it wasn't going to be reciprocal. At the same time, everything else in my life was falling around me. It was a friendship that I cherished but he was not really interested in being my friend. It was convenience more than anything.

I was suicidal every day; being bullied was at a peak. I never attempted suicide but I started thinking about self-harming. It was a way to cope and take my mind off whatever situation I was in. I felt I had no way out, no control over anything in my life so to try to self-harm was a very serious consideration. That's when the bullying was at a peak.

One day, I was walking home from school and two boys who were notorious for calling me faggot, gay, geek, and loser, followed me. I didn't take those words literally. They were just cruel words to say. On this day, everything changed, just like the day 'that woman' called me the half no one wanted. The two boys took their bullying out of the hallways and classrooms and followed me home. When I stopped to cross a street, they stopped.

I thought this was going to turn physical but they kept their distance. They kept calling names. By then, they knew I was crying. They could see the dots on the sidewalk from the tears, more ammunition for them.

When we got to my house, I remembered, thankfully, 'that woman' wasn't home yet. My dad, of course, wasn't home either. As soon as we got close, I ran. We had a slight hill in the front yard. I ran up the hill and behind the solid-walled front porch. I peeked over the wall and couldn't see them. I ran into the house, down to the basement and locked the door.

I could hear them upstairs at the front door. It sounded like a dog scratching to get in. I waited. When it stopped, I went upstairs. It was sunny outside and really cold. I looked at the front door. There was spit all over the glass front door, frozen. I panicked knowing 'that woman' would be home soon and it would be my fault.

I got window cleaner and paper towel and sprayed the window but that didn't work. The window cleaner just froze on the glass. I used my nails and tried to scratch off their spit. I was disgusted and felt so vulnerable. I wondered how I was going to avoid this, what would I do? This wasn't just a school thing, this was now at my front door. They know where I live.

I just wanted everything to stop. Everything was spinning out of control. I wanted to find a way to be in control. I wanted to stop the constant pain. I never did self-harm, but the thought of it helped me feel some control. I was getting more and more desperate.

One of my escapes was bedtime. I had a radio alarm clock and listened to a radio station called Chime FM. At nine o'clock, they always did the top five at nine. It was, for me, a kind of connection. It was like hitting the finish line. I knew that once I was lying in bed and the radio host came on, that meant the day was over. The bullying was over. The anxiety was complete. All that was left were my thoughts and those songs. It helped knowing I had crossed the finish line for another day.

Dream

Always, always, always, I dreamt of being a police officer. It was a very dominant thought for me from early childhood. It dominated my thoughts whether I was awake or asleep. That was my escape, to wonder what that would be like.

When I was young, it was about getting to wear a uniform, carry a gun, drive a police car fast with flashing lights. Towards the end of school, when I thought about being a police officer, it was more about being able to help people, to be in control, and to make a difference. I admired them. I thought, if I admire them, then people are going to admire me. I didn't know how many years it was going to take.

I had a fight with my dad one Boxing Day when we were driving home. It was a beautiful day and this guy was jogging down the side of the street. The back of his shirt read 'Police' and my dad said something like "I hate when people like that feel like they need to wear something that tells the world what they do." I got very defensive right away, and said "That's who he is. It's what he does". We got into a very heated argument.

His whole point was you do what you're going to do but you don't need to flaunt it. You don't wear it everywhere. "You don't see me walking around with a shirt that says I where I work", he said. I remember the moment. I remember what he was wearing, the white shirt and black track pants. It was one of the first times I went against what he said. I don't recall that I ever told my dad that I wanted to be a police officer. That was a dream that I held in for all those years. The argument with my dad was not about being a police officer but for flaunting who he was and I was standing up for this total stranger. I could feel myself changing. I was becoming a man. I was slowly getting stronger to the point of being able to disagree with my dad. I wasn't afraid to say what I was thinking. Today, I recall being impressed and proud that I stood up for myself. I was also afraid. I was afraid that I was going to upset my only real friend and support. If he turned his back on me, I was setting myself up for total isolation.

Around the same time, I was allowed to work at a part-time job at the front desk of a local hotel. One day, after being there for three months, there were two fires; one was in a sauna when someone left a towel over the wooden rack close to the heater; the second was at the top of stairwell where someone unrolled toilet paper and lit one end.

The police came and talked to me. The detective pulled me aside and held up a baggie with a pack of hotel matches and said "I know you set the fires." I was freaking out! I was so afraid and told him that I didn't set the fires. He told me he knew I set the fires because my fingerprints were on the pack of matches. I told him that I worked at the front desk and I hand out the matches! He said "No, no you set the fires. If you just be honest and say you set them, all you're going to get is probation, but if you say that you didn't set them and we have to go to court, you could be looking at going to jail." I was afraid to let the police officer down, and so, I said I did it. It was a false confession because I didn't want to disappoint the police officer and because I didn't want to go to jail. I was so used to taking the blame just to stop people yelling at me.

I went to my mom and stepdad's home. My stepdad lost his marbles. He screamed "You told them what?" I knew he was screaming more in disbelief than at me personally. I freaked out and told him I didn't set the fires and that I felt I had no other option.

On another day, like every day, after being bullied at school, the school bell sounded and school was over. I had to go home. I walked home nervous; it's repetitious. I got home and 'that woman' yelled so I went to the basement. She perched at the top of the basement stairs, shouting so loud that I knew at least the one neighbor could hear. I don't recall ever having said or doing anything to set her off. She kept screaming at me bawling in the basement.

After a bit, I saw the family car pull up in the driveway. My dad came in the side door and went to the liquor cabinet. He got his rum and diet Coke and came down to the basement. He stood in front of me with his rock glass with the ice cubes in it and stirred his drink.

She was still screaming. I'm still bawling and he stood right there. He took a few sips and said "What's going on?" It's like he was oblivious to her screaming and my crying and it took a long, long time but I looked at him and I said "Dad, she's screaming at me." He said the same thing as he always did, "just ignore her—she'll stop."

And then he did something he had never done before. He reached in his back wallet and gave me a $10 bill and said, "Tad, go out. Just go out for a couple of hours. Go play with your friends and then come on back later when everything is back to normal".

It was the start of something different. He had never given me money before. He had never asked me to leave the house. He never told me to go play with my friends because he knew I didn't have any.

I took the $10 and walked out the side door wearing only the clothes on my back. I started walking away. It was a Thursday night. I roamed around the streets for ages. After a time, I knew I had to go home, but my body physically would not do it. It just kept walking. At one point, I knew if I didn't go back right then, there would be no going back—I would be in such severe trouble.

In that moment, for me, there was no going back. For the first time, I was gone. Until then everyone I loved left me. This time, I was the one leaving.

These are the holes of the lock on the basement door.

This is the door that enters into the kitchen/living room upstairs. This door was like a vault to me and I don't remember a single time of turning that knob without my heart pounding out of my chest. This is also where 'that woman' stood and screamed down at me.

There were always shoes at the bottom of the stairs. They used to have an orange carpet wrapped around each stair. The window on the left, with the crumbling paint, is exactly as it was when we lived there.

This is the sink I peed into. My area was just to the left of the photo

The fridge was right below the window and my area was to the right of that.

This is the area where I sat. The one lightbulb and my only window are in the back corner

This is the door I walked out of when I left home. To the right is the lower part of the stairs leading to the basement

Out

I kept walking farther and farther away. I had nowhere to go, no adults to ask for help or couches to surf for the night. I roamed the streets all night long. Partway through the night, probably around 3am, the magic hit me.

There was not a soul out there that would come to help me unless I asked for help. I had to speak up and tell someone what was going on. For all those years, I expected that people would know that I was locked in the basement, that I was being bullied in school, because it was obvious to me. That night was the first time I realized it was not obvious to them. Bullying is a very secretive, private thing and I had to speak up for myself.

When the sun rose, I walked into a government office. I remember the ugly brown tiled floors of the welfare office. I walked in and went to the high counter and said I'd like to speak to someone please. A little while later, a lady invited me into her office and asked me "What brings you here today?"

I didn't manage to say a lot but I gave her the gist of what was going on in my life. Whatever it was I said that day, she believed me—and she believed in me. She agreed I was never going home again. So, they put me into a shelter and gave me student welfare. The intake process took a long time and at the end they gave me $475 a month. I had nothing but the clothes I walked away from home in.

There was no food, no appliances, no anything. There were four walls and a carpet. I had escaped the basement and all that bullying at home.

I was free to do whatever I wanted, whenever I wanted. There was no 'time for bed' or 'time to go to school.' There was nothing. I could have done anything.

I didn't go to school that day.

I realized I had to fix some things about myself. It was all up to me. I needed to keep this momentum going and as terrifying as this new experience was, it was an entirely different type of terror. The negative terror of living in that house was now replaced with a terror of the unknown and I could only trust myself.

The first thing I had to work on was to stop crying. It turned out to be the easiest thing of all. For all those years of crying, I truly, truly believed there was something wrong with me. I thought it would take years of therapy and that I was really, really messed up. It turns out, I was perfectly fine. The reason I was crying all the time was because I was terrified. I was petrified of 'that woman'. I hated her. I really did.

That Monday morning, I went to school. I didn't have to. No one made me, but I went. The boys started calling me names under their breath. I didn't cry, my shoulders didn't shake, the boogers didn't fall out like teardrops. Nothing happened. The boys went quiet for a bit. I focused on the teacher. They started again a little louder. They thought that I just didn't hear them. The fact was I did hear it but I had changed.

They had no idea I had been locked in a basement for twelve years. They had no idea of the challenges I'd been through emotionally and where I was, psychologically. They had no idea I had just run away and was now living on my own in the care of the government. Most importantly, they had no idea I was not afraid of them anymore. They kept calling me names but nothing happened.

I called my dad at work from a phone booth at school. He wasn't happy with me but this time, I was brave and I was strong. I told him I was not coming home anymore, just like my mom had told me all those years ago.

I told him to put all my stuff out on the porch and I would pick it up. He agreed. I asked if I could have the couch and table from the basement. He said no.

The police came when I went to collect my things, to support me by keeping the peace. They didn't get out of the car. It was same thing that we do today—we stand by and keep the peace. I didn't have much to get. There were some boxes and clothes, but nothing personal, no schoolwork, no school projects, no photo albums, nothing personal to say I existed before the age of seventeen.

My Mom lived close to the school and after leaving home, I saw her on a regular basis. All of a sudden, I had support all around me. The moment I found the courage to walk away from being bullied in the basement and stop reacting to the bullies at school, everything changed. I had an apartment, student welfare, and I had my real mother back in my life. And friends!

I went from victim to cool kid in one step. Because I lived on my own, I was now the cool kid. I had parties! A few of these new friends drove me to the house to get my things. They stayed in the truck. I didn't want to talk to my dad or 'that woman'. I didn't want to be put in a spot where I might cave emotionally. I had really matured within that first couple of weeks.

Around this time, I had to go to court about the fires at the hotel. The charges were dropped. It was very clear that I did not set the fires. Someone else was charged and convicted and all I wanted to say was "I told you so." But, 'that woman' told people that, from the bottom of her heart, she still believed that I did set the fires. There was no winning with her.

After the trial, my dad and 'that woman' came to mom and stepfather's to discuss what to make of me. My mom and my step-father said, "He's on his own. He's old enough now. He'll make his own decisions." My dad said he wouldn't pay for my lawyer for fighting this whole thing. I wasn't expecting him to. I said "How stupid do you think I am?"

They thought I was on downers. They thought I was on medication because I was so calm and so relaxed. The thing is they'd never seen me any other way because I was always crying in the basement. I've never been on any medication, not that there's anything wrong with that; I just hadn't. I had grown up years in a few weeks.

That was the last time that I remember seeing my father.

I started to develop friendships. I say friendship loosely because I had a lot of psychological trauma and I didn't feel like these people liked me for being Tad. I felt they liked me because I was cool, had my own place and threw some fun loud parties. I knew I was being used but it sure was better than being in the basement!

The pendulum had swung in the opposite direction very quickly. First, I stopped crying and then I learned how to say "hi." After the hotel fire fiasco, I got another part-time job at a local convenience store to afford the stuff I needed. It was a great way to learn how to communicate with people.

I become more extroverted but was still depressed and felt alone and untrusting. No one was allowed into that inner circle. Even today, I find it difficult to allow anyone too close.

I certainly wasn't ready to face the fact that I was living in a depressive state.

I finished Grade 13 at school on my own. I visited with my mom all the time. She was a big support and I had years to make up with her. I slowly furnished the new apartment thanks to help from my mom and my new friends.

Meals were nothing healthy, that's for sure. I have never been a fan of fruits, vegetables and milk, so mostly I ate meat and a whole lot of pasta. It was inexpensive. I had two pots, one frying pan and an oven roasting tray. The Dollar Store was my best friend. It was a great time, a frightening time, and I learned a lot about myself. I struggled with school and didn't go every day. I slept and just stayed home. I wasn't active. This was freedom—I didn't have to so I didn't. I knew I had to go to class so I went enough to make it work. My grades suffered but I still passed and I still graduated. I knew that high school was imperative to the dream of my future as a police officer.

Alcohol started becoming a big part of my life. I didn't turn to drugs. It was alcohol and only when friends came over. It was like the happy parties and drinking when I was a kid, except this time, I was throwing my own parties.

In my darker moments, my law teacher and his law classes really kept me going. Now that I didn't have to go home, I stayed and talked with him more after school. I don't know if I ever considered talking to him about what was going on. I suspect he probably knew something was up. I know I went way over the top, making dozens of tapes for him. It was my way of thanking him, of sharing the love I was so starved for. My grades were noticeably higher in his class than my others because I enjoyed his class. I am so thankful for him.

Tad 18 years

Tad 18 years

Letter

I sent a letter to my dad and 'that woman'. This is the first time this letter has been seen by anyone else. Here are some of the main points in the letter:

Mom & Dad

In response to your letter, I felt it necessary to speak from my heart and really tell you why I left. As you know, part of the reason was the rules and regulations, but there are several other reasons. Before I go into those, I want to once again say that the decision was mine. No one pulled my arm or encouraged me. Secondly, at mother's home, I was not on any downers to make me be calm.

* * *

I realize how you have tried to make everything very tough for me on my decision to leave home such as you intervening on my receiving social assistance or not giving me any furniture but I would like you to know that there is nothing you can do to prevent my welfare

Please note that I probably won't need welfare as I have 4 jobs possible for the near future.

* * *

4 unrelated friends
of yours have been in touch with me
helping me out with anything and
each have stated that there is a problem
in that house and quite frankly dislike
both of you for what has gone un-noticed
in that home.

* * *

I was alone in the basement with
no one to talk to or help me out when
I had a problem so I was forced to keep
it in.

* * *

So, being alone in the basement for 8
years, it's no wonder that my best friend
are the Blue Jays. Of course, when I
did have friends over, ▮▮▮▮ never hesitated
to mention me supposedly jerking off in
the bath tub as she indicated twice

* * *

There aren't enough
excuses in the world to cover what you
said and nothing you could ever say
can heal my hurt. I don't understand
how you could call this love?

* * *

I wasn't allowed to set it up for the past few years. The fact that there is no room is again bullshit because there was before. My liking to play baseball was constantly criticized because ▓▓▓▓ always said I wasn't any good. Yet, never once did she watch me play to say this. If I had a good test, there was always something else to cut up.

* * *

Something else that I have heard through the grapevine is that you both believe that I did start the fires at the hotel. Well, you have certainly drove the stake through the heart because to be honest, I will never forgive you for that. I did not start the fucking fires at the hotel. You being my so called parents should have been there to support me not go against me and play your damn games about paying for the lawyer one day and not the next. Just a minor point to add is that you can pay for my lawyer no matter who or where I live, I don't have to be living with you, Christ how stupid do you think I am?

* * *

I want you to know, that what you have done to that home is just brutal. And this isn't ~~not~~ just me talking. Does mental abuse ring a bell. It can be just as harmfull as phyical or sexual as I am just now finding out. Nothing was ever good enough for you. You have taken both of dad's son's away not to mention all of his friends. You ARE CONTROLLING HIM. You block out the fact that he is an alcoholic and can't see it himself. For 10 years I put up with what you call love. You can say that I am really mental but if you were to ask your "friends" they would tell you.

I have been told by 2 of your "friends" to change you and have a restraining order put against you both. This should be enough for you to see what you have done. You are dangerous. I can see that I have a problem and admit it. I think it's time that you did also.

* * *

And dad, please, please get some help with your drinking. You are an alcoholic. It runs in the family. I wish that we could keep in touch but I know she wouldn't let us. So, maybe one day when you can break her chains like I am we'll meet up again and can start over. I just wish that you had listened to my pleas to you and did something about it. Can't you see, you have lost both of you sons. You are the only reason that is making my leaving so hard. You were my best friend and you will be in my heart forever. I love you so much that I can't tell you. I just wish that you could see what is happening to you. I miss you so much and having that father figure (and best friend.) It is basically impossible for you to find out where I am so maybe in a couple of years when this dies down, I'll get in touch with you. Until then, like I said, I love you so much, and maybe one day, we'll meet up again. Barb, I think

you should look in the mirror and realize that it isn't the other people that are bad, it's you. Please leave my dad alone. I beg you. Keep the hell out of my life. You have done enough damage.

Goodbye!

Tad Milwin

'That woman' sent numerous letters apologizing to me at my birth mother's address. In them, she was trying to make me understand the difficulties of being a step-parent and wanting acceptance from me because I never really was her child. I think the letters were therapeutic for her but, even at that age, I knew there was nothing to respond to. I didn't want a conversation. It wasn't out of hatred. I just had no feeling.

At the end of school, everyone was trying to figure what to do and stressed about life, university, college, the workforce, where they were going to go, and how were they going to do it all. I was not stressed. Maybe it was because I didn't have any stress from home; I just had whatever was coming from inside me. The school gave us a questionnaire to fill out and it showed our top three career aptitudes. My number one job was police officer. No surprise!

When I graduated, my law teacher, gave me tickets for Tom Cochrane, who was absolutely huge back in the day with *Life as a Highway*. I sang that song like there was no tomorrow. And it was so neat to see my law teacher outside the school environment.

After graduating, I moved to a nearby town where my mom got me a job in a restaurant. She was a hostess and it was a great job. I finally made some true friends. We lived in a house where we partied a lot. I was still trying to look at girls, speak to them, and try to date them. I knew I was fooling myself because really, I was just interested in looking at boys.

I'd focus my attention on one boy that I wanted in my life. I pushed aside other friends. It was becoming a very big problem because I wasn't addressing what was going on with me. I didn't know how to deal with liking boys. There were no Gay Straight Alliances at school, no gay characters on television, no role models to tell me I was OK and show me how to express myself as a gay man. There weren't books to read in the library. I was not conscious of anyone who was gay amongst my friends.

I just knew I was different. I wasn't ready to announce I was gay. I wondered where happiness was. I couldn't find happiness no matter what I was doing. I just couldn't. I never felt the sense of belonging or being needed. I never felt love. I never felt close. I'd fight for something I wanted but it never felt reciprocal.

One morning, in my early twenties, I woke up. I mean I REALLY woke up! It was really cold outside; there was ice. I thought, "I'm done. I am outta here." It was time for something completely different.

I left all my belongings with my roommate, packed a bag, called my mom and said "I'm leaving. I'm moving to Vancouver", and bought a one way ticket to Vancouver.

Further out

I didn't really know Vancouver. I had visited there a couple of times and knew someone from work there. That was it. At Vancouver Airport, I told the taxi driver to take me $25 away from the airport. He dropped me at a mall in Burnaby, just outside of Vancouver. I got out and started walking. I saw a sign advertising a basement suite for rent and knocked on the door. The suite was furnished with a bed, a couch, a table, and cablevision. It was a really nice, little place, and it was available, so I dropped my bag on the floor of my new apartment and walked towards the mall.

A department store gave me instant approval for their credit card so I signed up and got a credit card with a $500 limit. I bought a television. I walked back to my new home, set up my television, and my new life began in a basement; but this time I got to choose a really nice basement…with cable!

I had one acquaintance who I had worked with at the restaurant in Ontario and he too had just moved to Vancouver. We hung out from time to time. I got a job at a restaurant.

A few months after arriving in Vancouver, I met a guy at the restaurant and started falling head over heels for him in a really demonstrative way. I was outgoing. We hung out all the time. We had an awesome time and did everything together, just the two of us. It was a tight friendship but not a healthy one because I had ulterior motives. I bought him trips and drinks and dinners out to buy this love. I wanted a relationship but had no idea how to conduct myself.

My love was getting more intense and the emotions were hitting me hard. This person wasn't going to fall in love with me the way I wanted. That's when I started cluing in—I was gay but had no idea what to do about it. My confusion put me back into that suicidal state which brought up memories of despair from my childhood.

After a time, I realized we weren't spending as much time even though I still made the time available for him; it wasn't reciprocal. One Friday night he told me he had something else going on and so we would not be hanging out as we usually did. I knew something was up so I went on this long walk around Burnaby until I found his very distinctive car parked outside a house party and he walked out hand in hand with a girl. He was gone and I was jealous!

I realized I didn't have much going on in my life. I had a job, an apartment, and a television BUT that wasn't enough for me. I was at my breaking point. I could not continue to live this way. I wanted to die and decided to commit suicide. I took a load of pills and went to bed. I blacked out; there was nothing.

The next morning, I woke up. It took me a while to realize I was actually alive. I had a really bad stomachache and called the doctor. I didn't tell him why I had this stomachache but I knew I needed to get my vitals checked out to be sure I was OK. In that moment, I knew I wanted to live. I no longer wanted to die. I just wanted the life as I knew it to change into something better.

When I woke up the next day—THAT was my awakening! I knew that my life had to be all about me and what I wanted. No one was going to make it happen for me except me. It was time to start recognizing who I am, both sexually, and as a person. I needed to love myself. I was very grateful that I was unsuccessful in my attempt to end my life. I look back on it now and it seems ridiculous to want to commit suicide over a relationship but it wasn't over the relationship. Really, I wanted to end being miserable and alone in my life and thought suicide was my only option. But when I woke up to find myself alive it felt like a gift of a new life.

I was introduced to another incredible young man and he and I hit it off really well. He was living with his girlfriend and was very committed to her until one night when he had little too much to drink, he got involved with another girl. His girlfriend kicked him out and he came to live in my little bachelor pad.

It didn't take much for me to become infatuated, and he and I became very close spending every waking minute together. I was repeating the same pattern with him that I had with others. After a while, we realized we needed a larger place to live. We talked to a friend at work and the three us got a house together with a pool table in the basement. It was great. Those were some of the best days of my life.

We each had our own bedrooms. Mine was the smallest bedroom. I liked the smaller confined room. My friend was down in the basement in a queen-sized waterbed and the other was on the other side of the house in his queen-sized bed. My friend didn't want to sleep in the basement by himself so I started sleeping with him every night. Without exception! I was down in the basement again, this time sleeping with a friend. We cuddled every night.

I was emotionally and mentally growing healthier. I was not comfortable with being gay and told him I was bi-sexual. When he didn't seem to care, I told him I was gay.

Now that I had told someone I was gay, I knew I had to tell my mom right away. Even though I had had a positive reaction, I was still hitting rock bottom and going lower because, in my opinion, my family was never going to accept this. I don't know why I ever thought they would.

So, on December 26th, I called my mom. I was nervous and said, "Mom, I need to talk to you." She said, "Honey I'm about to serve dinner—can it wait?" I swear I heard my heart bounce and hit the ground.

I was ready to say it. "Is it something to do with your health," she asked and I said, "No, my health is just fine" so she went to have dinner. She called me back and I said, "Mom you need to sit down, I need to tell you that I'm gay." She said, "I know" and I remember a pause. "What do you mean you know?" She said, "Oh, honey I'm your mother. When you were five years old, I walked in on you with two boys and I've known all along." She was laughing! I felt a sense of relief because I had said it, and we were still talking, so obviously she' wasn't going to abandon me. She was there, supporting me. My mom was NOT gone!

She shared with me afterwards that when she went up to the bedroom, and told my stepdad, he rolled over and said, "That's nice" and went to sleep.

That was it! No further discussion needed!

So now, I had told two people that I was gay. My friend was supportive but he still didn't budge on his interest in me. But he did invite me to travel with him! He said to me, that he had saved enough money to go to Scotland and wanted to backpack across Europe with no end date in mind. He asked me to join him.

Even further out

I had no interest in, or money for, travelling. He said, "I'll pay for you to come. I'll cash in my stocks and you can pay me back. Come with me. We'll go on this adventure together". I didn't really want to travel, but, when I realized that when he was gone, I would be alone again, so, I went to Scotland with him.

We used Edinburgh as our base. We lived it up in hostels and flats and had a great time meeting some incredible people. We got jobs and worked together in the same pub. It was great! And then, we decided to go to Prague for six weeks and that's when we started hitting a snag.

We camped on an island in the middle of the river in the centre of Prague. By now, I was in love with this guy and I always felt it was reciprocal except physically. I felt his actions, his conversations, his being with me 24/7 meant we were on the same page—after all, he just paid for me to go around the world with him! We had a really heavy falling out and cut the trip short by three weeks. It was ugly. I felt betrayed and then we made up. Emotionally, I was growing but was confused and hurt a lot.

And then, when we got back from Prague, we had another falling out and made amends again. Everything seemed like it was back to normal but he began pulling away. The flats we were staying at were monthly rentals and before, we'd always get the same room because it was cheaper but then he started renting two separate rooms. That was a bone of contention for me.

And then my friend met a girl who lived in London, a three-hour train ride away. He went down for several days at a time which would eat me alive. I was always extremely happy when he returned but I was miserable knowing that soon he'd be leaving again.

One time, he asked me to go down to London with him. I did and I was staying in the same room that they were. They were in her bed; I was on the floor not sleeping a wink. It was silent and I could hear the slightest movement like sheets moving and at that point I cracked and said, "I can't handle this anymore. I'm out of here." It was three or four in the morning. I got my stuff packed right then and there. I stormed out of the place and found my way to the bus station. I stayed there for the rest of the night and took the next bus back to Edinburgh. That was it. There was no repairing our relationship after that night. I was gone.

I stayed in Scotland; he moved to London. I stayed working at the pub. I had some incredible friends and never saw him again. I was okay. I'd gone through my depressive state with him. The night I cracked in London was just like when I cracked in Vancouver, the night I attempted suicide. This time, I felt heartache and knew I had to hit rock bottom before reaching the next great moment.

I went out for a lovely dinner with a girl from the pub we worked at. We had a huge bottle of wine, and we were having a great time. We walked out hand-in-hand and went back to her place. She turned out the lights and we started having sex. It was the first time I'd ever had sex with a girl and I remember being on top doing my thing and I started to cry. The tears were just dripping all over, but she couldn't see me in the dark so I faked an orgasm. I went to the washroom and looked at myself. I was disgusted with what I saw. For all those years I'd been the one who was hurt and that night

I knew I had hurt somebody. I knew she liked me and I had clearly led her on. I left. I had to do something. I couldn't keep doing this anymore.

I knew of a popular gay club in Edinburgh. One night I snuck away, even though I didn't need to. I was so hyper—sensitive that people would know I was sneaking into a gay club. I walked to the club with my heart pounding out of my chest. The music was great and the bar looked awesome. I got in the queue by myself and finally got to the door.

There were two guys, one on either side of the door and one of them stopped me. My heart was really pounding now. He said, "I'm sorry this is a gay club only—not gay friendly, gay ONLY" and I said, "I'm gay." It was the first time I'd ever said it out loud to a stranger!

He looked at me and said, "No, I'm not kidding. It's not for friends." I said, "No, I'm gay" and he said, "Prove it." One door staff looked at the other and said, "Kiss him." So I had my first real kiss, a quick peck with the door bouncer who wasn't very nice on the eyes. For them it was probably just a big joke, but that interaction changed my life!

I sat at the bar. I was uber-nervous and frightened but very proud of what I was doing. As I went down to the dance floor, the song changed to *If You Could Read My Mind Now*. THAT was the moment that it hit me—oh my God, look at all these other guys that were just like me. We all liked other guys. I wasn't alone! In that moment everything changed for me!

The next day at the very popular pub where I worked and where everyone knew who I was, I asked the DJ for the microphone and said, "Hello! Hello! I have an announcement". I heard "Shush, shush" from the crowd, "Canadian bloke is about to speak" and I said, "I just want everyone to know that I'm gay".

Absolute silence.

The first thing I saw was the girl I had slept with, bolting out the door. Then, in the far back area of the room, there was a single hand clap and it slowly spread til everyone was clapping. Everyone was very positive, very kind. I had handshakes. I had hugs. I had same sex kisses. One of my girlfriends gave me a huge hug and cried. That's how I came out. They're not kidding when they say the closet door opens fast!

After a while, I moved back to Ontario where I bought a house. I was successful working in restaurants and retail stores. I had come out in Scotland but I still wasn't happy. I just wasn't. I couldn't find true love. Or maybe I wasn't quite ready yet.

And once again, true to form, I ran. I packed up everything and moved back to Vancouver. I got a beautiful apartment. I got a great job as an assistant to a dean at the university. It was the best move I'd ever made and I have sure made a lot of moves. I knew I needed to do something and couldn't wait for someone to knock on my door. I needed to get out there.

I got involved in sporting groups; I joined a volleyball league and a baseball league. Neither of them turned into my dreams by any means, but they did result in some great friendships, social circles, and groups. I met a police officer named Shaun, on one of the teams. He worked at the Vancouver Airport. I told him about my childhood dream to be a police officer. He asked if I had ever applied.

I told him that no, I hadn't and rationalized that it was a childhood dream and that I was now too old. I was thirty two. Shaun looked at me and said something I'll never forget. He said, "Tad, one day you're going to grow old, you're going to reflect back on your life and you are going to remember you had a dream and that's it. Why don't you at least try? Give it a chance. You have nothing to lose and everything to gain. Then at least when you grow old you can reflect back on your life, remember that dream and say, "I tried"."

It took me several months after hearing his words to believe in myself enough to give myself that chance. I started envisioning myself becoming a police officer. I went to an information session where I learned that City Police required university training, but the RCMP did not. I applied to the RCMP.

I told my co-workers at the university about my dream and they were very supportive.

Tad in Scotland

RCMP

I wrote the RCMP test, received their package of what to submit, consisting of my resume, references, doctors' notes, and vision care. I did a lot of 'ride-alongs' with Shaun in Richmond and saw what the job really entailed; the paperwork, the driving, the isolation of being by yourself, going to calls by yourself. I was given an 'observer jacket' to wear. I had a vest and a flashlight and I felt like the bees knees getting in and out of a police car and. I was so proud of being identified with the RCMP and I wasn't even wearing a uniform. I was just so happy to be doing it.

It took me nine months from the day I wrote my exam to the day I got my acceptance letter. At our official registration at the RCMP detachment, the commander, welcomed us and asked us to introduce the person who had inspired us to join the RCMP. I was so bloody nervous I called him my dear friend Steve instead of Shaun! Everyone laughed so it kind of broke the ice a little bit. And within a couple of months, I was on my way to the RCMP training Depot in Regina with six other people from BC.

At Depot, everything was planned and recruits had to learn everything as we went along. We had to earn the right to march, to wear full uniform, even the stripe on our pants and boots.

In order to earn a boot or a stripe, we had to know about RCMP history. They lined us all up on Parade Square, in our red jackets, in the blazing sun. We were sweltering when they went through the line screaming at us, "Who was the third Commissioner in the history of the RMCP?"

We had to know everything and if we didn't, they screamed, "Get outta here" and then we'd go off as a troop. We'd have to study more, and try again the next day. Even once we earned things, they could be taken away. They made us grow up—they stripped us down and then built us up their way.

One day, our Drill Sergeant screamed at me. She said I had something green in my teeth and how dare you come here. I just stood there just looking at her and I kind of smirked a little. People started to giggle and again it broke the ice. I realized for as long as she yelled at me she was not yelling at the rest of my troop so, I was saving them. For a moment it felt like helping my brother to escape the basement.

And, in this case, I knew she wasn't yelling at me to bring me down like other people had. She was yelling at me to build me up, to make me stronger.

There were thirty two in my training group and I was the second oldest. I went to the RCMP Depot for one reason—I wanted my badge. I wanted to be a police officer. I didn't go there to make friends and I didn't go there to party on weekends. You get out of Depot what you put in. It's like life itself—you can get anything you want if you invest that time. I was focused; really focused.

For instance, at Depot, we had subdivisions with mock farm houses, a school, and police cars for us to use anytime. I thought about how we were doing all our training in daylight hours, when a good percentage of our actual job would be in darkness.

I got a group of seven or eight of us together, who weren't partying or going into town, to train on Friday and Saturday nights saying, "Let's put on uniforms, get those police cars and do some mock scenarios". I got my trainers to approve about fifteen practice scenarios and we acted them out and we had a great time. More people wanted to join in. At the end of training, one of the Corporals said we were less nervous and more confident in what we were doing.

I also hosted picnics; I bought food and invited people to meet at the campground on base. I invited them to donate a dollar a hotdog and then donated that money to the Fallen Members Fund. Everyone got behind that. I didn't know it then, but it was the first time I threw a party, asked for donations, and donated the money to a group I believed in. Today, I throw fundraising galas for *Bullying Ends Here*.

Other times we ordered twenty pizzas and brought horseshoes and bocce balls—anything to bring people together. I was so happy to finally be living my dream of being a police officer and having friends. I was nominated valedictorian of my troop and, for the first time ever, spoke in public. It was great to be recognized for going above and beyond. But really, I did it for myself, for all the times I didn't have friends because I was locked in the basement. I also needed everyone to help out which, in turn, helped them. This set up a winning pattern of bringing people together, helping each other, and doing something good for others.

Training was, for many, very difficult. Even when there were no classes, there was always something that needed to be done. I kept working because I knew that keeping that focus meant I could go to bed earlier at night. We were up at four thirty every morning and I was in bed by eleven, usually the earliest of anyone in my troop. I finished my list, my tests, and my physical training ahead of most of the others. I loved it and so I excelled. I was finally doing something I loved and was good at. I focused and then got to be even better. I ran five hundred and thirty two miles over the six months of training.

Running allowed me what I call, Tad Time; my peaceful time. I put my music on and ran. The basement and all those tears and all that bullying at home and at school were getting farther and farther behind me as I ran and ran and ran.

At four thirty every morning, I opened a can of diet Coke. I'd hear, "Morning Milmine". My bunkmates knew that the sound of the can being cracked meant it was time to get up. We had to iron our beds; everything in our closet had to exactly mirror every other closet. During random inspections, the Corporal took our caps and wiped them on the floor. Now, we couldn't clean those caps so we had to maintain absolute spotlessness at all times. If we didn't, the officer would mess up the room and we had to add that cleaning to the long list of nightly chores including polishing our boots.

It took about fifty hours of polishing to get those boots to the point that they can even be worn the first time. And, I loved it! It gave me something to focus on. I didn't have any external things like a wife and kids and bills. I was just living my dream of being a police officer. I was in the zone, and it showed, the whole time. I didn't struggle with the tasks we had to do. I did, however, work hard on my inner, personal struggles.

Being gay never came up. I didn't actively hide it and I'm sure people knew; it just never came up. I was so focused on doing everything I could to be the best police officer I could be. After dreaming about it for so long, I began to see how that dream really did save my life. It gave me something to focus on during my basement years. Running, physical activity and pure focus on the tasks at hand gave me the strength to stand up to the screaming Drill Sergeant. After being screamed at and called names all my life, I really felt my life was turning around and that dreams really can come true.

It was a relief to have a clear path and goals to achieve. I kept myself in the right frame of mind and ready to go. I found it enjoyable; it was the hardest, and most rewarding thing I've ever done.

At graduation, I don't actually remember receiving my badge it because I was so focused on keeping my steps perfect, remembering when to salute, where to stand, which hand to put my badge in and how to march away afterwards. It wasn't until later that night that it hit me that I was now a police officer. I had achieved my dream!

I awoke up the next morning to find that half the group had already departed. I had spent six months of every waking moment with them and they were gone.

So, in October of 2009, back in Vancouver, I was posted to the RCMP detachment in Surrey BC as a first responder. The first few times going out were challenging because there is so much to know like the roads, computer systems, policies and laws. Everything was so new. With time and repetition, things worked out.

Jamie

One night in late October 2011, I was reading the news on cbc.ca and a headline caught my attention that changed my life. It said something like "teenager takes his own life because of severe bullying." There was something about this boy, Jamie Hubley that struck a chord in me.

The article said that Jamie lived in Ottawa, and described the bullying that he experienced. It spoke about how he had a dream of being a figure skater and his family was very encouraging. They bought him figure skates, enrolled him in classes and Jamie went on to excel at the sport for years. He won awards and accolades, had a supportive family, and a terrific extracurricular activity.

The article also spoke about how Jamie was bullied by a couple of people in school. In the early grades, the abuse was mostly verbal like name-calling. Jamie knew not to give the bullies the reaction they sought; he kept his head high, smiled and walked away. Bullies seek reaction. It reminded me of doing this myself.

There was also a report of Jamie being punched by one or two people with the bystanders far outnumbering the bullies and how their role of inactivity played a strong role in the perpetuation of bullying.

As the years went by, the bullying escalated and shifted to cyber-bullying on the Internet. Jamie continued to keep everything in. He dug deep inside himself to look forward to the future. He looked forward to grade seven when he would change schools, and things would be different. It reminded me of how, in my dark days, I dreamed of being a police officer.

Jamie's first couple of week's at the new school was fine, but then the verbal abuse started at school and on the bus. Over the winter, it grew into physical harm.

One particularly bad day, Jamie's dad came home from work, sat down with his boy and asked, "Little man, what's going on?" Jamie managed to say "You know, they've been pretty cruel to me over the years", and then told him about three boys forcing him to swallow batteries. Another time, he told his mom that he swallowed the batteries on his own which would have been his first attempt at suicide. To this day, Jamie's parents do not know what really happened. All they knew was that their son needed help.

Jamie's mom took him to the hospital with a belly full of batteries. They said to let him try passing them for a week before they would operate. He did pass them! They got him mental health assistance to help overcome the traumatic experiences he had endured. They came up with plans, to help him move past all of this.

They agreed that when Jamie was ready, he'd go back to grade seven in a different school where all his friends from earlier grades attended. He would always have a trusted adult with him going to and from school for as long as he wanted these things.

But at this new school, one particular person bullied him and it was severe! It was a girl. She told teachers he was doing things he wasn't, to get him in trouble. She punched him and tried to get him off the school trip. Jamie's parents got involved and, enlisted the help of other students to convince the principal that Jamie was the victim.

To get through these dark times, Jamie looked forward to a different the future, this time to a new school in grade nine. The bullying continued. In grade nine, Jamie quit figure skating, thinking that if he quit figure skating, which is what everyone keeps making fun of him for, maybe they would stop. But the bullying continued.

His family saw that he wasn't going out as much, reverting to being by himself in his room at night, and writing on his blog. There's nothing wrong with being on the computer—there's so much to do on there and a lot of that is their social life. They play games or they're messaging. Jamie's parents weren't sure if something was wrong or if he was just being a teenager.

That summer, at the end of grade nine, Jamie opened up and told his family that he was gay.

Jamie's family was open-minded, and there was a lot of growing together, communicating and understanding that needed to happen and that's what they did. They all talked, all the time, about everything. Jamie started grade ten at the same school where he had been bullied all through grade nine– with determination, but not optimism.

He went straight to the principal's office and said, "I've been bullied for years, I've been in the hospital numerous times, and I want you to know. I don't want you to do anything because I've got a way to fix this." He explained to the principal, "the kids are not going to come up to me and be supportive in the hallway, locker rooms and classrooms because they're afraid if they get seen with me, they will be the next target.

I propose that you allow me to have a classroom for one hour, that's all I need. I want to tell everyone in the school that, on that day and in that room and at that time, I'm going to be available in private and if kids want to be supportive or give me a chance and see I'm no different to anyone else, they can come and say 'Hi'. I'm going to sit in that classroom and I'm going to wait for them."

The principal agreed.

Jamie made up posters to reach the 2,000 students that attended his school. He called his idea "The Rainbow Club" and he wrote the day, the time, and the classroom. He wrote, "Come and give me a chance, come and see for yourself that I'm no different than anyone else, just simply come and say 'Hi'."

He put the posters up all over the halls. The bullying continued. Relentlessly. But now the kids were talking about the event he was putting on. Jamie kind of took that as a positive, and saw it as a light at the end of the tunnel. He wanted to make a safe, supportive place that was open for everyone to come. As the week went on, Jamie noticed his posters slowly disappeared.

That Friday, the posters were no longer on the walls – they were ripped up on the floor. When Jamie's mom came to pick him up after school, she sensed that something wasn't right. Jamie said, "Mom, how's anyone supposed to know that I'm trying to do something positive if all my posters are gone?" Jamie's mom suggested that the family talk through the situation together when Jamie's father got home from work a few hours later.

When they got home, Jamie went to his bedroom and wrote an update on his blog. A short while later, Jamie's mom received a phone call from one of Jamie's friends saying. "Jamie just wrote something on the Internet that you should be aware of and you should probably go check on him."

When she went into his room, she saw lots of empty pill bottles. She ran outside and yelled his name but she could not see him in the field. She called the police, who said one of his friends had called them already. They were at her door in minutes. She called Jamie's dad who came right home. A massive social media campaign with a full emergency services search and rescue operation began with 100 volunteers. So many people loved Jamie and came to look for him. Later that night, they learned that Jamie had committed suicide.

When I finished reading Jamie's story, I was absolutely paralyzed in my bed. I was completely frozen, an experience I've never had before.

I had flashbacks of being a five-year old boy with a dream of becoming a police officer so I could do something positive to help people. My story was nowhere near what Jamie went through, but it was still there. And we both wanted to make a difference and help people.

Jamie's story reminded me that kids were still feeling alone, still needing someone to talk to; still looking for friends and protection. I had to do something, and I had no idea what. I knew one thing for sure – I had to do something positive for youth.

A few days after reading Jamie's story, I watched The Rick Mercer Report where Rick rants about politics, and things that bug him. His rants are usually funny. I had not expected to see anything serious on the show let alone about Jamie and bullying and sexuality.

Rick said that he knows firefighters, government officials, police officers and other people in positions of authority who are gay, but are not out. So how dare we tell people it's okay to be who you are if they're looking at us thinking you're not okay with who you are and giving mixed messages". I felt that Rick was talking personally to me.

I immediately told people at work that I am gay. There have never been any issues from my peers to my supervisors.

So, I have Rick to thank for that.

I later learned that Rick is a friend with the Hubley family. It is a very small world and we are all tied together.

The next step was to look up Jamie's parents, and sure enough, because Jamie's father works in politics, he had an email address online. It took me a while, but eventually I gathered enough courage and strength to put my thoughts into words, and I sent him email.

I told Allan, Jamie's dad, everything about me and at the end I asked if I could tell the world about his son. Can I tell anyone that will listen to me about Jamie? He responded within the hour, quickly and briefly—he's a man of very few words—"Yes" and then, "Good luck."

The first word was permission to share Jamie's story and the second his well wishes. I thought, "You know what? I am going to do something. Jamie put up posters and booked a classroom for kids to talk, now it's my turn. Jamie's story inspired me to try".

Jamie

Bullying Ends Here

I needed a name and that name would be my mission statement—*Bullying Ends Here*. Bullying won't end until we, as individuals, stop it ourselves. Bullying ends right here. It ends with me. It ends with each person who hears these stories and makes a commitment to themselves that bullying ends with them.

I created a website. It took me forever, because I didn't know how. I bought the domain name bullyingendshere.ca, I got the family permission, I felt ready to do something positive. I just didn't know what. The only thing I knew for sure was that it would be for youth.

At noon, on a day off, I went to the local high school and introduced myself as on off—duty openly gay police officer who had been bullied. I told them about the *Bullying Ends Here* website where kids could contact me and could I sit in on a meeting to see how things are in high schools these days. Total 'coincidence' their Gay Straight Alliance (GSA) was meeting and they invited me to attend. Perfect! I could get a feel for what is it like to be a student and part of a GSA which supports youth however they identify. My intent after that was to sit in the back of the class and just listen.

Instead, they asked me questions and not the questions I though kids would ask a police officer like "Do you drink coffee?" or "Have you ever shot someone?" They asked me, "How are you so lucky? How are you so fortunate to have gotten through that and to have achieved your dreams?"

They were looking up to me. I recognized right away that they weren't looking up to Tad; they were looking up to someone, anyone, who happened to be standing there. That's when it hit me—if they're trying to look up to someone, there must be other people out there as well.

I felt comfortable in front of them. I told them a little bit about my private life, things I'd never shared with anyone before, about being bullied, and about some of the challenges I'd grown up with. The teacher facilitating the GSA told another teacher who told another school and then the requests started pouring in. In 2012, I did a lot of presentations, all on my own time.

In late October, The Province newspaper in BC found out what I was doing and did a full page write-up including an archived picture of me in uniform. No one at work knew what I was doing—I hadn't told anyone, it was all on my own time. The Chief of the Surrey Police called me into his office and began saying he had no idea what I was doing on my days off. I explained that I hadn't told anybody because I wasn't looking for acknowledgments or recognition. I was just doing something that I believed might help others.

He said it was incredible and would I be open to the possibility of working this into my position as a police officer. It might mean doing it more frequently and not on my days off.

Around late November, he said he'd been able to work something out. If I was interested, I'd be working under the British Columbia RCMP's umbrella." This meant I'd move from the municipal RCMP level to the provincial level. Well, of course, I said yes! I already had some presentation dates set which they were willing to honour and so, I went to the provincial RCMP.

A week and a half into my new position, I sat down with my two superiors—the staff sergeant and the inspector and gave them the gist of what I was doing. I told them how I was fully booked until March in various cities within BC and Ontario. They hesitated—they're British Columbia RCMP, they can't pay for dates in Ontario. I offered to pay for Ontario on my own since I'd booked those dates long before I joined the unit. In the end, they found a way to pay for the Ontario dates and keep me on contract until the end of the school year in June. I did my presentations exactly as I had done before. I gave out the same *Bullying Ends Here* card with my own website and email address. Nothing had changed, except now I was being paid for my time and my expenses. It was a perfect relationship. I could focus even more on *Bullying Ends Here.*

During this time, I travelled to Ottawa to meet Jamie's family for the first time. My boss made it happen. The Hubleys welcomed me into their home, the home where Jamie had grown up.

At first, I was apprehensive and nervous. Jamie's dad, Allan, welcomed me at the door and warned me that two dogs would likely jump all over me. He offered me a drink. Jamie's mother, Wendy, joined us and sat on a chair by a wall that was basically a shrine to Jamie. They had his ashes, some photos, and some cherished family items on display. It was really powerful.

It wasn't just being in the house where Jamie grew up that had an impact. Now he was right there with me. I was trying to hold everything together. The two dogs, Elvis and Lucky curled up beside me, were calming.

Allan and Wendy were so kind and open. They were happy to talk about Jamie. Wendy shared some family photos and cherished moments…for hours. Elvis, curled up at my left, had bright, blue eyes, and every now and again he'd just look me up and down. There were moments of tears, and happiness and smiles and stories. As our interaction came to a close, Allan said to me, "I need to tell you something—those dogs, are Jamies' dogs, and I have never, ever seen them do what they did for the last six hours, just sitting beside you."

Before I left, Allan handed me a small parcel. It was a little unicorn lapel pin. In the last sentence Jamie ever wrote said, "I want to be remembered as a unicorn."

At Jamie's funeral, a person that Allan had never met before came up and gave him three unicorn pins. Allan kept one for me because he knew I could do something to make a difference sharing Jamie's legacy and that he knew that one day we would meet.

RCMP again

During this time, the RCMP had fully supported my anti bullying efforts. It was absolutely wonderful. At the end of May, my inspector told me my contract was extended for another year and that I could continue to give presentations as the demand increased.

I was also given a two page document to sign, describing the terms of what the next year was going to look like. The terms stated that I had to shut down my *Bullying Ends Here* website, that youth or anyone would only be able to connect to me through the RCMP website where someone else would monitor my emails. I was shocked! The whole point of the website is that youth can reach me at anytime and that it would be kept confidential. It is what I needed as a youth, and now what I was giving to the youths who needed it most.

The document continued to say that I would only give presentations inside British Columbia and they required approval from my superiors. Lastly, it stated, my days off could no longer support external anti-bullying initiatives. In other words, they were shutting *Bullying Ends Here* down!

I said no thank-you. It was all very pleasant, there was no animosity. I said, "Thank you very much. I'll finish the rest of June under your umbrella as the contract stated but then, I'd go back on the road and get back to being a police officer. I'll do *Bullying Ends Here* on my days off again in October."

A while later, I got an email saying my services were no longer required in the provincial units. The Surrey RCMP immediately welcomed me back on the road. They declined to honor the last month of my contract and sent me right back on the road. I knew they weren't feeling too happy about it but I was really excited to get back to the road.

I gave another presentation that June. I hadn't changed a thing aside from not wearing the uniform anymore. I was back in plain clothes, which turned out to be even more effective because the kids didn't know in advance that I was a police officer. They heard my story of growing up wanting to be a police officer and then they saw the badge; they knew I had reached my dream.

I was called back into the Surrey office in the summer of 2013. I had previously found a policy in the RCMP books stating that a member doing something positive for their community can request up to two weeks off with pay to do it. I had put a request in and they called me in for this meeting. My inspector and the superintendent, commended me for the work I was doing. I figured they were going to approve these two weeks. Instead, they slid a five page document across the table to me. It was an ethics complaint claiming I was using the RCMP brand to solicit funds. I had, at that point, not raised a dollar. I was extremely confused! I didn't understand how one day they were promoting my anti bullying efforts and paying for me to fly across the country, and the next day claiming I was in conflict with their policies.

It made no sense. I felt like I was in a black room with no way to escape. My experiences had taught me that all things work out by taking the 'high road', and not letting anger take hold of me. But this time, that didn't seem to be working. I felt the familiar pressure of having no choice, no voice and certainly no decision powers regarding where my career was going with the RCMP if I continued to work with *Bullying Ends Here*.

I looked over the fifteen points that to me were clearly misinformation. The ethics committee had never asked me to clarify information regarding the program or what was happening behind the scenes. It appeared to come from one or two people. I looked at my superiors and I said, "I guess I'm not going to be getting the two weeks." They were apologetic when they said, "This is over our heads. We're municipal. This is coming from provincial."

It was like being bullied all over again. For all those years of being bullied at home and then at school, I had held the future dream of being a police officer, and now I felt I was being bullied at work by two people who appeared to be trying to shut the *Bullying Ends Here* program down. I had always thought police officers were there to make positive change for others and now they were shutting down a program that did exactly that.

I had trusted them. As a child and a youth, I needed to trust them to help me get through all the bullying. This felt like a betrayal of that trust. It was an old pattern of dreaming a dream to get through the dark days, trusting a different future would happen, and now the old pattern seemed to be repeating itself at work.

The next morning at work, I saw the superintendent in the parking lot. Before I could even, say hello he said, "Tad, I need to apologize to you. Yesterday I sat in an office with you and served you with a document that was essentially telling you to shut your program down. I went back to my office and opened up the RCMP national quarterly and you were the centerfold—it's all about everything you were doing and at the very end, we're promoting your website." He says, "I need to apologize to you for everything that's going on because I don't understand this."

The RCMP does not have a union so I didn't have anywhere to file a grievance. All I could do was tell my own side of the story. I put together 57 pages consisting of four pages of my personal rebuttal and fifty three pages of supporting documents such as news articles, emails from kids, and emails from principals and teachers. As a police officer, I have been trained to provide all the facts. They handed it back and said it was too long. I rewrote it and submitted thirty pages. Every day, for four days, I was called in to the inspector's office. Ultimately the inspectors said they wanted to move past the ethics complaint and would I please submit a two page RCMP template document instead. I submitted my two page document. The ethics complaint was not spoken about again while they considered my rebuttal. I went back to being a police officer and heard nothing more.

Months later, with the ethics complaint still hanging over my head, the RCMP superiors called again, asking for information about the program so that they could get a better understanding to decide on whether or not they were going to approve my continuing with *Bullying Ends Here*. The calls were not about how the program works or how it was saving lives, it was about accountants and business licenses. I told them I didn't have an accountant because I hadn't raised any money. They insisted, so I gave them the name of an accountant. They asked for a City of Surrey business license. *Bullying Ends Here* is a nationally registered charity, not a local business. I tried to get a business license and was advised by the City of Surrey that a charity did not qualify.

I advised my supervisor who said, "It's going to come to a point where you're going to have to decide whether or not you want to continue doing this program while not being a police officer, or stop doing the program while being a police officer." Everything was going downhill and spiraling out of control.

Again, I had flashbacks of being bullied. It didn't matter what I did, it was never good enough for those who had authority over me. My dream of the police being there to help people was being shattered and my employer was acting as a bully just as 'that woman' did, and the kids at school had. How can a program called *Bullying Ends Here* on your own time, be bullied out of existence?

National

In October 2013. Allan Hubley, Jamie's father and Ottawa city councilor, invited me to a gala called "The Kaleidoscope of Hope" in Ottawa. It was a fundraiser for mental health, especially for youth, which Allan was co-chairing with Laureen Harper, the prime minister's wife. In June of that year, they had announced a new federal anti-bullying strategy, to train 2,400 teenagers across Canada in delivering peer education workshops and presentations against bullying for their fellow students—what an incredible honour! *Bullying Ends Here* was going national!

I got there the night before and I met up with Allan and Wendy. We went to the venue and saw how things were set up. Allan mentioned that I might be invited to say a couple of words.

The next night, we arrived early for a private cocktail reception and I was introduced to all these wonderful, influential people in Ottawa by Mrs. Harper—hockey players, politicians, a very elite affair. It was mind-blowing and wonderfully hectic. To me, the most important part of it was spending such quality time with Allan and Wendy, Jamie's parents.

When it was time for us to take our seats, I found myself at the head table sitting beside Mrs. Harper. She and Allan introduced the evening and Allan started talking about me. He said, "Tad, we'd like to welcome you up to the stage." Thank goodness I'm not shy! I walked up and he said, "Tad, we want to present you with our first ever award from "The Kaleidoscope of Hope", for the work that you're doing with *Bullying Ends Here*.

After presenting me with this honour, Allan asked me to tell my story to the crowd. I took to the podium and I just started talking. Until that day, I had never had the opportunity to speak about Jamie with his parents present.

I spoke a little bit about everything I was doing and I looked at Allan and Wendy who are now sitting at the table; I said, "I can only hope that in your time of tragedy, you can see that something positive is coming out of it. There is positive change taking place, and I hope it brings you some comfort."

When I finished and returned to my seat, there was a draw for grand prize. The draw was set up with a locked door, and there were 150 keys sold that might open it. The key that opened the door was called "The Door to Paradise", the grand prize. Everyone lined up to try their luck. I was talking with Mrs. Harper—she was so eloquent and kind. The line-up got shorter and shorter and people were beginning to wonder if anyone had bought the winning key. There were only five people left in the line and a lot of people were standing there with cameras, knowing the winner would be announced any moment now.

I remembered that I had bought a key on my way in. Mrs. Harper asked, "Why didn't you get up in line?" With my luck, the person in front of me would open the door but I stood up anyhow. A collective murmur rippled through the audience, because I had just given my impromptu speech.

I walked up to that door and lo and behold, my key opened that door! I went totally numb—how I remained standing, I don't know! I've never won a dollar in my life before and here I was with such important people in one room, all because of Jamie. I was speechless and could only look up and say, "Thank you Jamie." I knew that he had played a role in this. How else could I explain winning such a luxurious prize when I had never won anything in my life? The keys that were purchased were all mixed up on the table when I purchased mine, so there was no way to rig it. I looked back at Allan and Wendy—it looked like they had tears in their eyes. The audience roared.

The grand prize was a trip for two to Jamaica's top rated resort in a private hut over the water. I was so focused on *Bullying Ends Here*, that I couldn't make the time to take the trip, so I sold the tickets and put the proceeds towards the program.

Tad with Allan and Wendy Hubley at Kaleidoscope of Hope in Ottawa

Tad and Laureen Harper at Kaleidoscope of Hope in Ottawa

Adrian

Adrian

*A*drian was my partner, and one of my best friends. We met when we joined the RCMP in Surrey and hit it off right away. We worked the same shifts and went to the same calls. He had a wonderful personality, always smiling, happy and animated. He had a beautiful girlfriend named Shelagh and the three of us spent a lot of time together.

In November, Adrian booked a night off to surprise his girlfriend with tickets to see her favourite country band playing in Seattle. He worked the night before and would have finished at 4am, but decided to work later knowing the team was short staffed.

Around 6am, my phone rang. I saw it was one of my line mates and I ignored it, thinking it was pocket-dialed. The phone rang again—another line mate. "Did you know that Adrian was just killed?" I wasn't awake enough to process this horrible joke—I didn't think that it could be real.

He said, "Turn on the news. He's been killed in a car crash." That's when the messages started coming, people phoning knowing that Adrian and I were so close, knowing that I really needed to know right away, especially before I turned on the television.

I had to go to the scene—I just had to see it. It's one thing to see something on television but everything I see on TV at home is not reality to me. Television is just television so I needed to go there myself.

The road was closed for blocks all around as the collision happened in the middle of a very busy intersection. The area was eerily quiet. Way down the road, I could see a transport truck turned awkwardly and sitting there, not moving. I couldn't see anything else so I began to walk the two blocks to get closer. As I got closer I could see what appeared to be the backside of an unmarked Police vehicle. My nightmare was slowly becoming a reality with each step closer.

Adrian's car was severely crumpled in the front, especially the driver's side. The door had been pried away, most likely from the firefighters who had worked so hard to free my friend. There was no one around me as I simply stared in disbelief. I knew it was Adrian's car as he always loved to drive the unmarked vehicles. I just knew it was true, Adrian was no longer with us.

I slowly walked away, trying to catch my breath and grasp this new reality. I went to my vehicle and drove to our headquarters where the team was meeting. I don't think I remember that short drive at all; I was completely numb.

Headquarters was close to the scene so I went up there and found everyone crying and numb, like walking zombies. No one really knew what to do. I wasn't crying. I was more concerned with supporting the first responders.

We all pulled together as a family. It brought us all closer together. It reminded us that being a police officer can be over in a matter of a moment. Adrian died on impact—fortunately, he didn't suffer.

I remembered that about a week before he died, Adrian and Shelagh had come to a school where I was speaking. Afterwards, the kids crowded around as they usually do to say "Hi" and share a story. When they left, Shelagh gave me a huge hug. She had tears in her eyes. Her long hair brushed up against my face as she leaned in and said, "He loves you, you know—he's proud of you."

Adrian came up to me, so animated and full of life, and said "Buddy! I had no idea this is what you're doing on your days off. When's your next one?" I told him it was a larger one in a theatre. He asked me to save two seats for him and Shelagh—they'd love to come again.

It turned out that was the day of Adrian's funeral. I knew that Adrian wanted me to do that presentation. The school offered to reschedule, having seen the story on the news and knowing it affected my team. I kept the engagement.

It was a very somber event. Everyone knew who I was, although they didn't know the connection between Adrian and me. The principal got up on stage and introduced me. She pointed out the two seats that the school saved for Adrian and Shelagh. I joined her on stage and before I began, I thanked Adrian, and told the crowd how Adrian and I were partners, and that all of my favourite calls were with him. I said "When I'm done here, I will be rushing to his funeral."

After the presentation, traffic was all backed up, but I had to get to the arena. I was an honourary pallbearer and I was running late. I think I broke all the rules of the road possible to say goodbye to my best friend.

When I arrived at the arena, I was met by the others for his procession who went out of their way to help me get into my ceremonial uniform. I don't think they understood the need to still do the presentation that day but they accepted it. I knew that I had to do it for the youth and for Adrian.

We all formed up by the hearse and then it started. There was a sea of red along with hundreds of other agencies present to show their respects.

The entire funeral took about seven hours. It was like no one wanted to say goodbye and wanted to be with him as long as possible. The last time I would see Adrian was as his hearse was driving away, surrounded by a motorcycle police escort taking him to his final destination. I just watched for as long as the road allowed as they all sped off.

When I got home that night, I sat on the couch and was absolutely wiped. Totally wiped. I opened up my computer and saw over three hundred and fifty emails from the youth at the presentation in the morning. At first, I thought it was a mistake! It wasn't. Most wanted to share their condolences and say something kind like "we can't believe what you did", "thank you so much for coming", "loved the presentation", "so sorry to hear about your loss."

With every email I read, I knew I was doing the right thing. Now I had two people looking down on me and guiding me, Jamie and Adrian. I wear two bracelets every day, one for Adrian and one for Jamie. It was an incredible moment. One moment feeling alone and then the next having hundreds of messages of support.

I always mention Adrian in my presentations. I want to bring home that as police officers, we take a pledge, when we receive our badges, that we will sacrifice our lives to protect and defend those around us. Adrian gave the ultimate sacrifice. While everyone was sleeping, Adrian was doing his job to save and protect his community.

RCMP one more time

*I*n March of 2014, I was called back into the Surrey RCMP office. My senses told me something was up so I asked my supervisor to accompany me to the meeting. He had been so supportive. We had played out every scenario of how this might end up going, so I knew there was potential that this day was going to end badly.

We walked into the office. The new superintendent was there. As soon as I sat down my inspector started off, "What you're doing it's great. You know we support you. We stand behind you. We know you're a terrific police officer—but there are some things we need to talk about."

They both had books in front of them with some pages sticking out. They served me with a two page Cease and Desist order along with three pages of supporting RCMP policy. It stated very clearly I am to 'cease and desist' all emails with youth, shut my website down, cancel future presentations and deny any media requests—effective immediately. I required final approval from the RCMP to continue doing *Bullying Ends Here*.

"Sir" I said respectfully, "When I'm done with this meeting today I'm going to go home and respond to all those emails from the kids that have messaged me today. Tomorrow I have a presentation and I will do that presentation. I'm going to disobey your direct order, so what's the next step?"

He said, "Please don't put us in that position."

I said, "Sir, I am a [expletive] great police officer, nominated by my peers for Police Officer of the Year, twice. I attend more calls than anyone else and have never had a complaint. When I'm done in this meeting I'm going straight to the Chief's office and handing him my resignation—effective immediately. I cannot work for a place that doesn't recognize the importance of resolving bullying, especially outside work hours. We have to open our minds and move forward". I quit on the spot.

I couldn't believe the same thing was happening again. First it was my parents, then it was the kids at school and the police officer and the fires, and now it was happening again. I trusted their authority to have my best interests at heart, and again they did not. And once again, it was all up to me to defend my dream.

I went to Laura Balance of LBMG, a media contact who had been incredibly supportive of my work and asked what I should do. She suggested that we take the story national right away—get it out there and get it over with. She said it would swamp me for a day or two, and then dissipate. The other option, she said, would be to NOT publish the story in the media. She said that the story would come up everywhere I did a presentation, as the media always attends in every city. I would have to explain the situation over and over, thereby continuing a story that I just wanted to end. I chose to take the story national. I want to say a big thanks to Laura for believing in me and supporting me when I needed it most. We have a wonderful partnership and even better friend.

I gave an interview to the Province newspaper. They put it on the front page with an archived photo of me in uniform. It described how I was harassed and how I was, in their words, bullied out of the force for doing an anti-bullying project.

When the story broke, I had the darkest feelings I'd had since my teenage years. I felt like, all of a sudden, the world hated me. I received angry emails and social media messages. I felt very alone. I gave interviews to all the television and radio stations that asked. The newspapers followed suit. A day and a half later it was done—the storm had passed.

Big thanks to Laura for believing in me and supporting me when I needed it most; a wonderful partnership and even better friend.

Senate

And then, just a few days after leaving the RCMP, I flew to Ottawa to be recognized in the Canadian Senate for my 'honourable work'. I stood in the Governor General's box while the speaker read all the things I have done to end bullying and the senators stood and clapped for me. It was humbling, awesome, and confusing. I had just been forced out of my position at the RCMP and now was being nationally recognized in Ottawa. It was really, really confusing!

While I was doing presentations on my own time, I came to Calgary for a week to do a tour of Calgary schools. Two weeks before the tour, I got an email from Constable Andy Buck, Diversity Resource Team, Lesbian, Gay, Bi-sexual, Transgender, Queer* Liaison Officer, Calgary Police Service (CPS) inviting me to meet him while I was in town.

Calgary

It's not uncommon for the local police service to attend my presentations, to know what is being said in case someone comes forward to them with questions. I responded back and Constable Buck came to my first Calgary presentation. And then he came to every presentation I did in Calgary. One day, between presentations, he took me up Scotsman's Hill, overlooking the stampede grounds. It was a beautiful cold, sunny day with a blue sky and white puffy clouds. "It's beautiful," I said, "I could see myself living here." "Be careful what you wish for," was his reply.

I applied and began to learn about Calgary. I did a couple of ride-alongs and met the higher-ups. They offered me a job. They knew I had to fight for what I know to be true, and, right up to the Chief of the Calgary Police Service, they wanted me on board. I could continue being a police officer and do *Bullying Ends Here* on my own time.

The Calgary Police Service recognizes there's not just one way to resolve bullying. There is a lot of information available to youth by all policing and community service agencies, based on facts, videos and handouts. That's not the approach I take. I tell my story and I tell Jamie's story and invite them to say "Hi". There is an emotional connection.

Not everybody wants an emotional connection, especially with police officers who are often seen as devoid of emotion. We're just supposed to know everything, get it done and save everybody, but the reality is that we all have feelings. We all have emotions. Police officer or not, we all cry, we all love, we still get angry. We're all humans.

Tad and Constable Andy Buck in Calgary

Tad and Rick Hanson, Former Calgary Chief of Police

Tad and Rick Mercer at World Pride Parade in Toronto

Tad and Justin Trudeau at World Pride Parade in Toronto

Brian Burke, Mayor Nenshi, Jon Cornish, Tad, Andy Buck, John Fennell at Calgary Fundraising Gala

Tad and Leslie pre-launching this book at
Calgary Gala

Tad, Tad's Mom, and Stepdad

Bullying Ends Here continues

S ince then, *Bullying Ends Here* has been receiving amazing support and exposure. The program has been coast to coast across Canada 6 times reaching over 150,000 youth in hundreds of schools. Dozens of requests have been received from around the world.Over 25,000 emails have been received and personally answered and 32 lives saved!

I have marched in the Toronto Pride Parade with Brian Burke, President of Hockey Operations for the Calgary Flames and a long—time supporter of gay rights in sports. I've met Olympic athletes and hockey players from both the Toronto Maple Leafs and the Calgary Flames. Brian Burke introduced me to my personal inspiration, Rick Mercer, Canadian comedian known for CBC Television comedy shows, This Hour Has 22 Minutes and the Rick Mercer Report. It was his two minute rant on gay rights and bullying that propelled me into action *Bullying Ends Here.*

I've established a relationship with, Laureen Harper, the prime minister's wife, Justin Trudeau, leader of the Liberal Party of Canada, Senators Grant Mitchell, and Mobina Jaffer, and multiple members of federal politics.

The most humbling invitations continue to be from the schools. They invite me in to present to two, three, four thousand kids at a time. The invitations come from all across the country.

Bullying Ends Here held its first fundraising gala in Calgary on 21 February 2015 with 150 people in attendance.

Headlining the event were Brian Burke of the Calgary Flames, Jon Cornish, running back for the Calgary Stampeders and John Fennel, Canadian Olympic Luge athlete who came out during the controversial Sochi Olympics. The event was hosted by CTV, and opened by Calgary's Mayor Nenshi. Also in attendance was *Bullying Ends Here* board of directors.

For three weeks in the spring of 2015, I toured eastern Canada giving two presentations a day to schools in the Atlantic provinces and Ontario. I also was invited to speak alongside the Chief of Police in Toronto at their Pink Shirt Day event and later attended a Blue Jays Game.

I am at a good stage in my life. I am enjoying life in Calgary and am now ready to explore dating opportunities. Time will tell how this, and the next chapters in my life, sort themselves out.

Basement revisited

I took the opportunity to drive by the house I grew up in. The current owners were sitting on the porch. I walked up and told them who I was. They very kindly invited me inside. Upstairs had been completely redone and it was beautiful.

My old bedroom was just the same as I remembered it. The closet still has the sloped ceiling and same shelves as when I was there. The room felt the same size as when I was there.

Approaching the door at the top of the basement stairs was powerful. It was closed and we stood outside of the door for quite some time talking about it. There was a chain lock on it but the small hole from where the lock was when I was there was still visible. In fact, the current owners said the lock was there when they first moved in.

The basement was exactly as I remembered it; it had the same musky smell to it; the dents in the wall were still there with cement falling apart from the original cement not being perfectly poured. The layout was, of course, the same. The basement ceiling seemed lower (I have clearly grown!). The fridge was not there.

As a child I was told a man in a straight jacket lived in the basement and was terrified to go downstairs. After years of being forced to live in the basement, I was terrified to go upstairs. Even today, the current owners call the basement 'the dungeon' and don't like to go into it. So much time has passed and I have come such a long way from running away and getting my own place. I graduated from high school on my own, I have lived in different cities in Canada and Scotland. I am out as a gay man and am living my dream of being a police officer. And, I speak to tens of thousands of youth every year through my program, Bulling Ends Here.

Going back to the basement where it all began, and with a very different perspective, I know that if I can do it, you can too. It is important to get help when you need it. I am speaking out to stop bullying, and you can too.

Message

My message isn't just about bullying; it's just about being an all-round good person. It's about making dreams come true and making the world a better place. Whatever an individual decides to take away from it is up to them.

My hope is that if you feel the way I felt, like you don't have anyone to talk to or to pat you on the back when you deserve it, that you'll understand that there are people around. I never knew that I did, but it turns out I was wrong. I did have them—I just didn't know it.

By speaking from the heart, I hope you see that you are not the only one that feels that way and people really will help. It might be too late for me, too late for Jamie but it is not too late for you.

Reach out to me. Let me know. I'll talk to you every single day. I'm happy to. I'm honoured to. That's what the whole message is.

I never knew if that day was going to come for me. It presented itself when I was 17 and I just kept walking. I walked away from the darkness of the basement into the rest of my life. That's not to say that running away is the answer—but it is what brought me here.

Although I have a story to be told, truth is, many more chapters are still to be written. I have told my story to date and found a way to turn it into something positive. Life throws us some curve balls at times but it is up to us to deal with them. Life hasn't always been easy but it is my life. I am proud of who I am and that includes what I have been through. Although I cannot change the past, I can live NOW and work to ensure that tomorrow is much better.

Tomorrow I will be better. Tomorrow I will make a difference. Tomorrow I will be someone's hero.

Testimonials

"…thank you for the great presentation that you gave our kids. I want you to know that you have affected many of the students and that your name has been used in my office many times over the past couple of weeks. The kids see you as a true role model that they can look up to."

TEACHER

"I wanted to send you an enormous Thank you!! You gave a presentation at my son's school yesterday. He talked to me about your presentation all the way home from school, but nothing more. This morning he went into the school and asked to have a private conversation with his Learning Coach and he "told" all. I received an amazing phone call shortly after.…"

PARENT

"Your presentation made a difference in our school. Within a week of the presentation a few students came forward to me about the bullying that had been happening to them for almost a year. The bullying was happening both online and in person. I wanted to let you know that the student who was bullying is now being dealt with and the kids who are bullied are feeling much more safe. Thank you for making such a difference in the lives of so many people."

HEALTH CARE PROFESSIONAL

"I appreciate you sharing your story with us today more than

you could imagine. You've have completely opened my eyes and I've come to realize that there's always a light at the end of the tunnel. Thank you so much for coming today, I hope that eventually everyone in Canada has the opportunity to experience your presentation because it unlike anything I had ever heard before. The message that you've shared with us is something I know will stick with me for ever. You give people like me hope for the future and I'll never be able to thank you enough do that. Today's presentation was something I'll never be able to forget."

STUDENT

"I just want to thank you so much for saving my life. Your presentation showed me that there is light at the end of the tunnel. Because of your presentation, I've opened up to adults and am now getting treatment for two eating disorders, self-harm, depression, anxiety, and PTSD. I also struggle with my sexuality, and your talk helped me see that everything will get better. Maybe not today, maybe not tomorrow, maybe not for a month, but one day. You are an amazing man. Keep doing what you do. I can't thank you enough."

STUDENT

"In one short hour you were able to accomplish what I have been trying to accomplish for many years!!!"

PARENT

"I have been a public educator for 34 years and as a school principal for 25 years. I must say that I have never observed a more powerful, compelling presentation than Bullying Ends Here."

PRINCIPAL

"Thank you so much. You've inspired me so much these past

two days. I went to my counselor at school and there was a positive change. Telling an adult has helped. Thank you. :)"
STUDENT

"Usually when (my son) comes home he says hi Mom and we chat for a minute or two, he gives his one word answers, then he disappears to his room or the basement. However, today he came home so moved by your story. We talked for at least 10 minutes. He told me so much about your life and the hardships and how you have overcome so much. He talked about the young boy who was an ice skater who committed suicide. He talked about the moment you told the kids that you were gay and how their opinions of you didn't change. He really admires your courage and strength and your ability to share your story. This is my son, who rarely says more than 10 words, who just kept talking about you! I just thought you should know you are changing lives and you are making a difference in the world. Way to go Tad."
PARENT

"My son met you last year and subsequently contacted you. This contact was the beginning of an entirely new chapter for him. He was in a very sad place last year and I really didn't know how to help him. I am happy to report that he is doing very well—best start to a school year ever. He is involved, confident and happy. I can't thank you enough for being there for him—he really related to you and you treated him like an intelligent and mature friend, which made all of the difference."
PARENT

Hundreds more are listed on bullyingendshere.ca…

Tad Milmine

Having been neglected at home, bullied at school, and struggling with his sexuality for many years, Tad has now achieved his dream of being a Police Officer, a dream he held close to his heart since the age of 5. Having read about the suicide of 15 year old Jamie Hubley, Tad created the charity, Bullying Ends Here. Tad gives presentations to hundreds of schools across Canada each year sharing his own story of resilience and inspiration to thousands of kids. To get involved and/or donate, please visit bullyingendshere.ca.

Tad lives in Calgary, Canada

Acknowledgements

I would like to take this opportunity to thank a few very important people in my life.

First of all, thanks to my Mom and Stepdad (Dad) who have been there to support and accept me. You are both so amazing and I am proud to call you my parents.

I would also like to thank Leslie for all of your time, professionalism and expertise in putting this book together. To see my life in a book, from my perspective, is quite extraordinary. None of which would be possible without you.

I would also like to thank my best friend, Andy Buck. You have been my rock since the first day I came to Calgary for a presentation. I would be remiss if I didn't thank the Senior Staff of the Calgary Police Service for believing in me and allowing me the opportunity to continue achieving my dream of being a Police Officer while continuing to help make this world a better place.

Lastly, I want to thank the Hubley family for welcoming me and allowing me to share your son's story with anyone who will listen. I truly hope that the positive changes coming from the presentations, and this book, bring you some form of comfort to know that lives are being saved.

Tad Milmine
April 2015, Calgary, Canada

Leslie Robinson

Living by the quote, 'be the positive change you wish to see in the world', Leslie has taught in colleges and universities for 25 years. She has authored and published 30 books in diverse fields such as tourism, education, metaphysics, facilitation, business, survivors of torture, and now anti-bullying. Leslie collaborates with authors to write and publish best selling books. To continue the conversation, please visit leslierobinson.ca and teachingtourism.com.

Leslie lives with her partner in Calgary, Canada.

Acknowledgements

It has been my honour and pleasure, to work with Tad on *Bullying Ends Here: My Story*. Your passion, determination, and non stop emails have kept us in constant contact from the recording of your stories, editing the transcriptions, clarifying dates and events, and obtaining photos in six drafts over six months. Your story is changing lives and making a positive change in the world. Thank-you for who you are and all you do, Tad. Let's continue to make a positive change in the world!

Thank-you to my amazing team including Elisha Pierre who transcribed the voice recordings so professionally, and quickly. Warmest thanks to Chris Burkhardt for your helpful word suggestions, grammatical corrections, (especially the tenses!) and for hanging in there with technology and visitors. Thank-you, Mary Scobie, for your patience, calm clarity, and graphic skills in laying out both the eBook and print copies. And a very big shout out to Vanessa Dunae for your thoughtful questions and suggestions in the much needed 'hard edit' and your gracious, tenacious, and exacting edits in the more subtly-nuanced soft and final edit.

And thank-you to my partner, Jane Oxenbury, for your interest, for your editing and especially for making space in our lives and home for this book to be birthed.

Leslie Robinson
April 2015, Calgary, Canada